LOVE
MUMBAI

A HAND-BOOK FOR THE LUXURY VAGABOND

LOVE TRAVEL GUIDES

Second Edition, 2008
Handcrafted in India.

Love Travel Guides is
a registered trade mark
of Hardys Bay Publishing

Published in India by
Hardys Bay Publishing Pvt. Ltd.,
Bangalore, India

ISBN 978-81-904322-2-1

Printed in India on eco-friendly,
non-bleached, hand-made paper;
with the entire production process
child labour free. More publishing
notes available on the last page
of this publication and on our
website below.

LOVE TRAVEL GUIDES
www.Lovetravelguides.com

LOVE
MUMBAI

I believe falling in love with a city is just as exciting as falling in love with a person. Your senses become engaged and you simply feel more alive...

LOVE TRAVEL GUIDES
www.Lovetravelguides.com

LOVE
MUMBAI

Preface

The intention of this guide is to introduce
you to the most authentic experiences in
Mumbai so you can fall in love with this city.
The selection criterion was easy – does the
place help one fall in Love with Mumbai?
If yes, it was in; if not, it was out. For every
entry that made it, many did not.

All entries are based on merit, with no
payments or incentives involved.

Special thanks to all of the *'Bombayites'*,
'Bombaywallahs' and *'Mumbaikars'*, who shared
their Love stories with the city with me so I
could include the special experiences you will
find in these pages.

Change is inevitable, please let me know
if you come across any outdated information
and also any suggestions for additions at
fiona@lovetravelguides.com

For updates and to be part of the
Love Travel Guides community, please
register at *www.Lovetravelguides.com*

Happy journey,
Fiona Caulfield

India, January 2008

MUMBAI & BOMBAY – A TALE OF TWO CITIES
by Anand Giridharadas

This megalopolis on the Arabian Sea is India's epicenter of business and entertainment. It is a city of mind-bending extremes, where $8 martinis coexist with eight million slum dwellers. It is the city of Asia's oldest stock exchange, the world's most prolific film industry and some of the priciest apartments on earth.

It is also a city hopelessly two-named.

A version of this essay first appeared in the March 1, 2005, edition of the International Herald Tribune.

It has been more than a decade since India's wealthiest state, Maharashtra, sought to purge a colonial legacy by rebranding its flagship city as Mumbai.

Has the new name stuck? That depends.

To some, Mumbai is a fait accompli. *"Nothing will come in the way of the new name,"* said Yashwant Sinha, a former foreign minister in the Bharatiya Janata Party. But a taxi driver from Sinha's home state, Jharkhand, had another view: he had not heard of it. *"Whether there's been a change or not been a change, I don't know,"* said the man, who settled in the city in 1993. *"We people have said Bombay from the start, and we'll keep saying Bombay."*

The receding of colonial empires and the fall of Soviet communism sprinkled new names across the world map. Some (St. Petersburg) work better than others (Myanmar), but Mumbai is particularly vexing. If the outside world still wonders what to call it, it is because the city itself has no answer. Ask as many people as you like; it is impossible to judge whether the rechristening has succeeded or failed. It has, in fact, done both with panache. It is rare to find Bombay on the lips of a bureaucrat or the address of a parcel. It is equally hard to catch a taxi driver or investment banker uttering Mumbai.

Bombayites and Mumbaikars have agreed to disagree. But this much is clear: if Mumbai was intended to repaint a many-hued city in the monochrome of postcolonial pride, it has instead shown Bombay to be richly polychromatic. Name chaos is testimony to the city's unique, working-class cosmopolitanism: the live-and-let-live ethos of the crowded street. Bombay and Mumbai have become indicators of the city's kaleidoscopic diversity. Every vocation, ethnicity and neighborhood has its preferred usage. Bombay versus Mumbai is a sociological litmus paper, revealing to which of two parallel cities you belong.

Bombay is the city of seekers. It has long attracted outsiders – merchants and migrants, Christians and Muslims, Indians from all over. They have brought big dreams, shared tight quarters and learned the mercantile ethic of tolerance. It is the city of shopkeepers and industrialists long established, and of laborers and professionals recently arrived. Their Bombay is open-armed and rootless. *"This city belongs to the entire nation,"* said Amit Badaskar, a Maharashtrian taxi driver.

Mumbai, by contrast, is the city of the rooted. Once home to the fishermen from whom Maharashtrians descend, its openness increasingly corrodes their traditions and sidelines them from power. It is the city of working-class Maharashtrians and of the political establishment they elect. Their Mumbai is proud and rooted.

Though the membrane between these cities is permeable, there are plainly two realms, of Bombayites and Mumbaikars, where one name slips out more readily than the other. Yet Bombay's magic lies in line-crossing, in taking pains to use a name suitable to someone else. A city of 17 million people sharing a slender, reclaimed island is a city acquainted with adjustment. To live in Bombay is perpetually to adjust – in its trains, lanes and cramped apartments.

Mumbai connotes seriousness and respectability, Bombay frivolity and glamour. Thus the *Times of India*, a national newspaper, writes Mumbai on front-page datelines, while branding its widely read entertainment insert *Bombay Times*. Mumbai connotes public purpose, Bombay private gain. In government meetings, big industrialists are sure to say Mumbai to placate high-ranking mandarins. But on its own letterhead the Bombay Chamber of Commerce and Industry refuses to go by Mumbai.

Ninety-seven per cent of intra-city mail uses Mumbai.

Mumbai is what you write, Bombay what you say.

"When you fill up forms, then you go with Mumbai," Malini, a middle-aged woman scanning titles at a Bombay bookshop, told me. *"But when you're talking to someone, it's definitely Bombay."*

The city is like a bride with a new surname, writing Mumbai in formal letters but letting Bombay slip out in speech.

A business executive might convene a meeting in Mumbai, but she will summon a lover only to Bombay.

Foreigners are baffled. Briefed on post-colonial sensitivities by guidebooks, they arrive with Mumbai rolling off their tongues. Then, moving through elite circles, they notice that no one else is saying it.

The world shares their hesitancy. Air tickets say Mumbai, but luggage tags read BOM.

Yet if outsiders are perplexed, the city's own embrace two-namedness. *"When I write, I write both,"* Sujata Patel, a sociologist, told me. *"Everyone uses both names in the streets of Bombay,"* she said. *"So why should we be different?"*

Notes

I MUMBAI MUST'S

Briefing:

Mumbai is the biggest, wealthiest, and fastest city in India. Often compared with New York in terms of its energy, Bombay also is a city that does not sleep – the famous lyrics 'If I can make it there, I'll make it anywhere' also hold true of Bombay. The similarities continue with the high-rise sky line. I have borrowed from Manhattan an idea to name South Bombay, SoBo and North Bombay, NoBo.

This 437km square island city is densely populated and simply understanding how the city works and plays is fascinating. Here is what I believe you 'must-know' about the city and also the recommended 'must-do's'. Enjoy!

Must-Know's

Must-Do's

MORNING

DAY

EVENING

Must-Know's

City of the Sea

The city began as a small settlement of fisher folk, the *Kolis*, who worshipped the mother goddess *'Mumba Aai'* or *'Mumbai Devi'* (the inspiration for the city's name change in 1995). With growing prosperity, the city grew through land reclamation, the original islands becoming a single land mass and now continues to expand across the harbour with Navi Mumbai.

Ganesh

The Island of Good Life

Vasco da Gama discovered the direct sea route to India in the late 15th-century and in 1634, the Portuguese were *'given'* the seven-island archipelago and proclaimed it to be an *'Ilha da boa vida'* with cheerful reports of beauty and abundance. In 1661 the King of Portugal gave the islands of Mumbai to King Charles II of England as part of the marriage dowry of his daughter.

'Bombay is a Crowd'[1]

The population of Greater Mumbai is 19 million, bigger than 173 countries, and is *predicted to become the world's most populous city by 2020.*

1. *India: A Million Mutinies Now* by V. S. Naipaul

Ganesh Mania

Ganesh, the god of new beginnings and the remover of obstacles, is the patron deity of Mumbai (and of writers). *Ganesh Chaturthi is the biggest festival in the city,* celebrating the birthday of the much-loved god. Held annually in August/September, over the 10-day festival close to 10,000 Ganesh statues are paraded on the streets before being taken to the sea for immersion.

City of Empire

The East India Company leased the city in 1668 and it soon became the centre for west coast trade. By the mid-19th-century Bombay was booming, cotton mania was in full force; after London, it was the biggest city of the Empire. Splendid Neo-Gothic buildings were constructed including the Victoria Terminus, the University, and the High Court.

Home to the Indian Railway

The first train journey in India took place in 1853 from Bombay to Thane and carried 400 people. The Mumbai commuter trains, running on three lines, now transport over six million people per day.

City of Gold

Always a market place and counting house, *Mumbai is now the commercial and financial capital of India.* The Bombay Stock Exchange is the oldest exchange in Asia and the second largest in the world. Mumbai is home to 40% of India's wealthiest business people, real estate is more expensive than Manhattan – Mumbai alone pays over 38% of the nation's taxes.

Asia's Largest Slum

Spread over 175 hectares, Dharavi in Mumbai, houses over one million people. 54% of Mumbai's population live in slums, where most inhabitants exist in one-room tenements. Dharavi is at the heart of small-scale industry in Mumbai, with an annual turnover of US$665 million.

Bollywood vs Hollywood

Bollywood began in Mumbai in 1899, about a decade before Hollywood, with a film called *'The Wrestlers'* shot in Hanging Gardens. Bollywood makes 1,000 films a year, double Hollywood's output.

Fashion Capital of India

Mumbai makes full use of the Bollywood glitterati to showcase its wares. *Fashion Week* takes place twice a year, Spring/ Summer in March and Autumn/Winter in October, and is now an important fixture on the global fashion calendar.

City of Three Seasons

Latitude 18° 56 " N, Longitude 72° 51' S, Altitude 3m. *Mumbai has three seasons – Winter* (Nov - Feb) is very pleasant; *Summer* (March - mid June) is hot and humid and the *Monsoon* (mid June - mid Sept) is when Mumbai gets a lot of rain. On July 27, 2005, Mumbai had 37 inches in one day.

Crime & Punishment

'Bombay's menace is not street crime. It's bigger and more organised than that.'[2] Best-selling books, *Maximum City* and *Shantaram*, expose the Mumbai underworld in all of its complex glory. Bollywood was funded by it, celebrates it on celluloid, and now has some its most famous stars in Arthur Road Jail. Mumbai is a city of riots and bombs; drugs and prostitution; where extortion payments are tax deductible; and police *'encounter'* (assassination) teams are legendary.

World City

'A city of perpetual immigration.'[3] Mumbai has long been regarded as a meeting point for the world, an amalgam of the best and worst of both the East and West. It is a magnet for people of many races, religions, castes, and languages from all over India and the world.

City of Dreams

The steady movement, estimated to be over 300 families a week, from the villages to Bombay is about dreams. The dream of becoming a Bollywood star or simply having a better life, getting work, making money and gaining freedom from the cages of caste, gender, and religion.

2. *Maximum City* by Suketu Mehta
3. *City of Gold* by Gillian Tindall

Mosque & Temple

The scenic Haji Ali Mosque is located on a little islet off the coast at Worli. It is reached by a 500-yard narrow causeway, lined by beggars and accessible only at low tide. Next go to the 200-year-old temple at Prabhadevi, one of the most popular Ganesha temples in the city. On Tuesday, the most auspicious day, there are serpentine queues, which foreign visitors can skip. *Inside the temple make sure you whisper your wish into the mouse's ear.*

Must-Do's

MORNING

At Sea

Arrive at the Gateway of India at dawn to see the gaily coloured ferries bathed in pink light. Then make the ferry crossing to Elephanta Island to see the 4th-century cave temples.

Day at the Races

Head to Gallops *(pg20)* for breakfast on race day and enjoy the social scene of the turf club. *Derby Day* is the peak event held annually, in February.

Morning Markets

Visit Sassoon Market to see the *Koli* fisher folk bringing in the catch and then off to historic Crawford market to see the abundance of fresh fruit and vegetables. Wonderful in the mango season of June and July. Then off to Café Madras *(pg21)* for a delicious South Indian breakfast. If short on time, head into Badshah *(pg26)* for a juice and a snack.

Sunday Service

The Afghan Church, built in 1847, is one of the prettiest in the country, tucked away in the Colaba woods. *The Remembrance Day service is quite special, complete with Indian bagpipers.*

Marine Drive & Malabar Hill Meander

Join Mumbaikars on their ritual stroll along Marine Drive and head up to Malabar Hill. The Jain temple on Ridge Road is beautiful and has spectacular views. Then head to peaceful Banganga tank, one of the most important spiritual places in the city.

DAY

Dabbawallahs & Dhobis

See how Mumbai lives and works. Be outside Churchgate Train Station at noon to see the Dabawallahs delivering over 150,000 lunches. Harvard, Princeton and Yale have studied them and Forbes gave them a Six Sigma performance rating. Next go to the Dhobi Ghat to see the biggest open-air laundry in the world with 5,000 Dhobi Wallahs, all men, pounding the city's washing clean.

Bazaar Day

Mumbai is a shopper's paradise and nothing beats the energy and the magic of the bazaars and markets (pg82). Make sure to visit the Mumbadevi Temple, named after the same goddess as the city and then enjoy the best *thali* in town at Shree Thakker Bhojanalay *(pg22)*.

Train Journey

Chhatrapati Shivaji Terminus (formerly Victoria Terminus) is one of the world's grandest train stations. Board a train to Matunga and emerge, 20 mins later, in South India. This charming area has garlands of flowers for sale, temple bells happily ringing and truly excellent food. Lunch at Ramanayak Udipi Shri Krishna Boarding *(pg18)*.

Village Life

Take a stroll through the lanes of Khotachiwadi, visit the Ferraria house *(pg99)* and then have an early lunch at Anant Ashram *(pg19)*.

Cultural Safari

Choose your art galleries *(pg71)* and antique shops *(pg68)* then recharge at Café Samovar *(pg19)*. Make sure to see the Sassoon Library and the sky blue synagogue nearby.

Old Bombay

Take a walk past the maidan, the University and the High Court. Visit the grand museum. Make time to visit the graceful and time-less Asiatic library and then lunch at Café Britannia *(pg22)* in historic Ballard Estate.

Gandhi House

Mahatma Gandhi lived at Mani Bhavan from 1917 to 1934, and from here he launched the Satyagraha movement and learnt to spin using a *charkha*. Afterwards head to the nearby By the Way Café *(pg27)*.

EVENING

SoBo

Glam

Sunset drinks at The Dome *(pg33)* followed by dinner at Trishna *(pg28)* and then for the glitterati scene more drinks at Indigo *(pg34)*.

Real

Sunset at Chowpatty to soak in the scene, followed by dinner at Shalimar *(pg29)*, dessert at Taj Ice Cream *(pg32)* or at Bachelor's *(pg32)* on the way home.

Colaba Night

Stroll along Colaba causeway market, catch a Bollywood movie at Regal Cinema *(pg106)* and then head for an evening of beer at Leopold *(pg33)* or Mondegar *(pg33)*.

NoBo

Glam

Sunset drinks beach side at Vie *(pg40)* and then to Don Giovanni *(pg40)* for a sensual Italian dinner and off to Enigma *(pg41)* to party.

Arty Juhu

Sunset drinks at Sun'n'Sand, a show at Prithvi Theatre *(pg105)* then a coastal dinner at Mahesh *(pg38)*.

Bandra Night

Drinks at Toto's Garage *(pg40)* and the Hawaiian Shack *(pg40)* in Bandra, dinner and some good music at Soul Fry *(pg40)*. A nightcap at Zenzi *(pg41)* to finish.

Planning Map

This map is to assist you
in planning your Mumbai
experience by showing the
areas of the city where
entries are located.

For ease of navigation,
we have divided the city
into **NoBo** and **SoBo** and
have defined 25 areas.

Throughout this book, city
entries are coded accordingly.

Alphabetical Index (pg150)

Area Index (pg154)

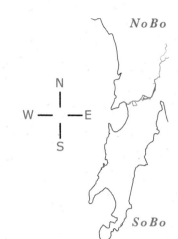

NoBo

N
W — E
S

SoBo

North Mumbai
(NoBo)

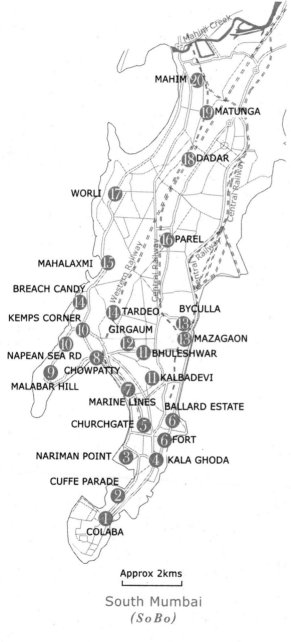

Approx 2kms

South Mumbai
(SoBo)

Notes on Getting Around

Know a landmark – this is vital, as having a street address is not enough to get to your destination. Landmarks could be temples, police stations, offices, shops or traffic signals.

Get connected – a mobile phone is a 'Must-Have'. Often you will be 'guided in' to your destination. Also make sure you have your driver's phone number.

The Eicher City Map – get this terrific book; detailed, accurate and easy to use. A bargain at Rs.250. However, be aware that only you will use it! Drivers won't ever use a map and will continue to stop and ask locals for directions.

Mumbai takes time – Mumbai is one of the world's biggest cites with woefully inadequate infrastructure. The North – South axis is hugely busy and clogged, *traffic-choked roads are common.*

Avoid rush hours – Double your journey time if travelling between 9am - 10.30am and 5.30pm - 9pm.

Puri bhaji, bhelpuri, you can try and tell
Idli dosa, hot samosa you will like it well
Once you come to stay
then you won't like to go away
Come to Bombay, come to Bombay
Bombay meri hai.

Bombay Meri Hai! lyrics, Mina Kava and Naju Kava
from the anthology, Bombay, meri jaan

LOVE TRAVEL GUIDES
www.Lovetravelguides.com

IIa DELICIOUS
SoBo Dining:

Mumbai seduces you in many ways, most powerfully through your sense of taste.

A meeting point of culinary traditions from North and South India, eating here is like taking a culinary tour of the whole country and, increasingly, the world.

With several hundred thousand restaurants and street stalls, you can eat anything and anywhere. Snack on the sand, eat on the street, visit charming historic cafés, and frequent the country's most glamorous restaurants.

Take delight in India's gourmet capital.

NoBo Dining:
(pg35)

Eating ('Day')

Eating ('Night')

Drinking

*'Day' and 'Night'
descriptions are
subjective, as most
places offer all-day
service. Mumbaikars
eat late, 9.30pm
is normal and
reservations are
recommended.*

Eating ('Day')

BEST EATING ADVENTURE

**⑲A Ramanayak Udipi
Shri Krishna Boarding**
1st Floor, LBS Market Building
(nr Matunga Central Railway Station).
Ph: 2414 2422, 3290 0282
Daily 10.30am-2.30pm, 7pm-10pm.

The city's first Udipi restaurant was established in 1942 in Matunga, the south Indian enclave in Mumbai. Easily reached by a local train from VT, get a first-class ticket and enjoy the 20 min journey to another world.

Freedom fighters were regulars and today celebrities and locals mingle happily. Curious foreigners are welcomed. The owner also eats at the restaurant and rarely misses a meal. He explains that his father told him not to sell what he couldn't eat himself, so he serves food that is like his mother's cooking. The place is immaculate and the food delicious.

Vegetarian fare is served on plantain leaves or on plates. The plate version is limited (Rs.21), the leaf version (Rs.55) is unlimited. Items include steamed rice, rasam (a spicy thin lentil soup), *sambar*, chutneys, vegetable curries, spiced rice, fried *vade* or dumplings, butter milk or yoghurt/curd and a sweet. *Note you are expected to eat with your fingers, but a spoon can normally be found!*

Café Samovar

BEST LOVED

④ Café Samovar

Jehangir Art Gallery, Kala Ghoda.
Ph: 2204 7276
Mon - Sat 11am - 7.30pm.

The much-loved bohemian Samovar has had artists and intellectuals grace its doors since 1964. A narrow corridor of a café located at the back of the gallery, it is always buzzing with conversation and great energy and is the ideal place for a snack, coffee or beer. Its stuffed *paranthas* (flat breads) are famed.

Sit underneath the whirring fans with the crimson golden lights and the greenery outside – this is a romantic place, in every sense. Great stories have started here.

Look out for the book *'The Making of Samovar: How a Mumbai Café Became a Metaphor for a Generation'* written by Usha Khanna and her daughters, Devika and Malavika, in an effort to garner support for the café's existence which is currently under threat from closure by local authorities. Artist Rekha Rodwittiya wrote: *'The greatness of every city is measured by the quaint old institutions that stand the test of time and weave their magic in the comfort they offer'.*

Here's to Samovar standing the test of time for many generations ahead!

⑫ Anant Ashram

46 Khotachiwadi, Girgaum (arrive at Charni Rd Station, get off on the east – the side away from the sea, and take the laneway opp the Old Majestic Cinema on Girgaum Rd and ask for directions!).
Mon - Sat 11am - 1.45pm,
7pm - 9pm
Arrive early, they often run out of food!

While finding Anant may not be easy, a wander through the narrow lanes of Girgaum lined with 19th-century Portuguese style villas will transport you back in time.

There is no signage for the restaurant and no menus once you are there, however this spartan restaurant has been giving Mumbaikars fabulous coastal cooking for over 80 years. *Communicating with the staff is hard work, so you need to be prepared – well worth the effort!*

Every customer sits at a separate small, marble-topped table and is served promptly with the best of Maharashtrian coastal cuisine.

No alcohol is available, so have bottled water or try the *sol kadhi*, a sour-spicy drink made of kokum fruit and coconut milk, spiked with green chilli.

Tempting as it is to have a room service breakfast or to simply pop downstairs to the hotel dining room, it is worth making the effort to have a Mumbai breakfast adventure.

The city is at its best in the morning, before the streets are choked with traffic and when the locals are relaxed and getting ready for the day. The food is also terrific.

BREAKFAST
(*ONLY IN MUMBAI*)

🅑 Gallops

Mahalaxmi Race Course, Mahalaxmi.
Ph: 2307 1448
Daily 6.30am - 9.30am, noon - midnight.

On race days, breakfast starts early and is served alongside the track. Jockeys, owners, trainers, and the odd horse mingle in the garden enjoying a robust breakfast. Make sure to check out the schedule during the season, which runs November through to April. A full listing is at www.rwitc.com, the website of the Royal Western India Turf Club.

🅵 Olympia Coffee House

Rahim Mansion, Colaba Causeway.
Ph: 2202 1043, 2204 5220
Daily 7am - midnight.

Tracing its history back to 1940, this Muslim café is a much-loved Colaba landmark. Lined with mirrors, it features marble-topped tables and straight-backed wooden chairs. Olympia is famed for the *kheema baida pav* (lamb mince with eggs served with a bun) and the *behja* 'brain' masala. *Not a place for vegetarians!*

🅶 Sassanian Boulangerie

98 Anandilal Podor Marg, Marine Lines
(nr Gol Masjid and Liberty Cinema,
close to Bombay Hospital).
Ph: 2200 6198
Daily 7am - 11pm.

This well-worn Irani café is a good option for a simple breakfast of coffee and an omelette (chillies and onion optional) or an afternoon snack. The *mawa* cake, a buttery rich cupcake-like confection, and *brun maska* (buttered bun) go down well with a cup of steaming Irani chai infused with mint.

Another Irani café worth trying is:

🅶 Kyani & Co

Jermahal Estate, Near Metro Cinema.
Ph: 2201 1492
Daily 6.30am - 9pm.

SOUTH INDIAN BREAKFAST

⑲ Café Madras

38b Circle House, Kings Circle, Matunga.
Ph: 2401 4419
Tues - Sat 7am - 2.30pm, 4pm - 11pm.

This humble eatery is the most-respected
place for authentic south Indian food in the
city. The famous *dosas* (paper thin pancakes)
are served with *sambar* (lentil and vegetable
curry) and spicy fresh coconut and green
chilli chutney. Try the *masala dosa* with savoury
potatoes stuffing, the *neer dosa* made tender
green coconut water and meat, or the nutri-
tious *raagi dosa* made from red millet flour.

Others to try:

⑲ Sharda Bhavan

LN Rd, Matunga East,
(opp Matunga Central Railway Station).
Ph: 2414 1271
Daily 7am - 8.30pm.

A charming old café. Good dosas and lovely
traditional tumblers of South Indian coffee

⑲ Mani's Lunch Home

Dabbawala Sadan, (opp Shankar Math Temple),
Telang Rd, Matunga.
Daily 7am - 10.30pm.

A no-frills café serving good south Indian
food consumed to the sound of cheerful
temple bells.

POWER BREAKFAST

③ Tiffin

The Oberoi,
Nariman Point.
Ph: 6632 5757
Daily 6.30am - 11.30am.

If you are out to impress,
or want to mingle
with business tycoons
and film moguls, choose
this modern, stylish café
off the lobby of the
Oberoi Hotel.

COMFORT BREAKFAST

① Indigo Deli

5 Ground Floor, Pheroze Bldg
Chhatrapati Shivaji Maharshi
Marg, Apollo Bunder
(between Regal Cinema
and Gateway of India).
Ph: 6655 1010
Daily 9am - 12.30am.

An offshoot of the famed
restaurant Indigo, this stylish
contemporary deli and
patisserie serves high-quality
comfort food all day
and evening.

Thali

Named after the flat plate and little bowls in which it is served, thali is a full Indian meal. It includes vegetable curries, lentils, rice, breads, papads, yoghurt chutneys, pickles and sweets; while the dishes change, the concept is the same across the country. The most popular thalis in Mumbai are the Gujarati, Marwari and Rajasthani. Thalis are usually eaten with fingers (right hand only) which allows you to assess the temperature of the food as well as appreciate the textures of the food with the fingers as well as the mouth. Alcohol is not served.

LUNCH

⑥ Café Britannia

Sprott Rd, Ballard Estate, Fort
(opp New Customs House).
Ph: 2261 5264
Mon – Sat 11.30am - 4pm.

This historic Irani café lives up to its motto *'There is no greater love than the love of eating.'* Famous for its berry *pulao*, made with *zaresht* (Iranian barberries), Café Britannia is a great place to sample many Parsi dishes like *salli* chicken and *dhansak*. Make sure to leave room for pudding, the crème caramel is "to die for". *Full of old world charm – a 'must-do'.*

⑪ Shree Thakker Bhojanalay

31, Dadyseth Agiary Marg
(opp GT High School), Kalbadevi.
Ph: 2201 1232, 2208 8035
Daily 11am-3pm, 7pm- 10.30pm. Closed Sun Dinner.

Nestled into the busy market area, this 60-year-old restaurant deserves the effort it inevitably takes to find it. Without a doubt the best Gujarati *thali* in town. The air conditioned first-floor restaurant is calm and has high standards of hygiene. The menu changes daily and a regular *thali* will cost Rs.130, the elaborate Sunday *thalis* cost Rs.150.

THE REST

⑪ Rajdhani

361 Sheikh Memom St
(opp Mangaldas Market, nr Crawford Market).
Ph: 2342 6919, 2344 9014
Daily noon - 4pm, 7pm - 10.30pm.

Located in the heart of the fabric market, this small train carriage size restaurant serves a great *thali*. Wednesday is Rajasthani *thali* day.

⑦ Golden Star Thali

330 Raja Rammohan Roy Rd
(opp Charni Rd Station, near TBZ).

Fresh, fresh, fresh – no food kept more than two hours. *Not a tourist in sight, this is a Mumbai foodie favourite.*

GUJARATI

Gujarati cuisine is often called haute cuisine for vegetarians. Two places compete for the best Gujarati in Mumbai and are excellent for sampling, in safety, all of Mumbai's best street food. Both are great lunch spots.

⑭Swati Snacks

248 Karai Estate, Tardeo Rd, Tardeo
(opp Bhatia Hospital).
Ph: 2351 0994
Daily noon - 10pm.
(limited menu and hot drinks 3pm - 7pm.

This 42-year-old family run restaurant was recently given a stylish make-over and it is now even more popular. It is full of Mumbaikars, ladies-who-lunch, families, teens – all enjoying traditonal, inexpensive Gujarati cuisine.

Go hungry! Try some of the best pani puris in town and the signature *panki chatni* (thin pancakes in banana leaf) and the rich and luscious *dal dhokli* (whole wheat *roti* cooked in Gujarati dal). *Don't let the long queue put you off – it moves quickly and you can always opt for the take-out window instead.*

⑧Soam

Sadguru Sadan, Ground Floor,
opp Babulmath Temple, Chowpatty.
Ph: 2369 8080
Daily noon - 11pm.

Opened in 2005, Soam offers vegetarian Gujarati and Marwari cuisine similar to Swati. *To taste a wide range of food, ask for the explanatory English menu and try one of the excellent platter options.* Bright fresh décor and whitewashed walls make this a terrific place for a light lunch or a snack. Healthy options are noted and there are some good juices and simple coconut water to accompany the meals.

VIEW

①Souk

Taj Mahal Palace & Tower Hotel, Apollo Bunder, Colaba.
Ph: 6665 3366
Daily 12.30pm - 2.45pm,
7pm - 11.45pm.

Souk has a view over the Gate of India across the Arabian Sea; this elegant restaurant captures the romance of the sea and of the mysterious Orient. At night the restaurant is romantically lit and quite sensuous.

Good Middle Eastern cuisine is prepared by two chefs from Beirut; try the mezze platters. For a very special experience, arrange for the seven-course meal at the Casablanca table in the Souk Kitchen. The Sunday buffet brunch is also very popular.

AFTERNOON TEA

①Sea Lounge
Taj Mahal Palace & Tower, Apollo Bunder, Colaba.
Ph: 6665 3366
Daily 7am - 11.45pm.

The Sea Lounge has borne witness to many marriage plans and introductions. It is a calm spacious room with wonderful views out to the Gateway and is a perfect place to dream of adventures across the sea.

This serene matron of Mumbai effortlessly moves from breakfast to lunch to high tea to evening drinks. Enjoy the most hygienic (and most expensive) versions of the classic Mumbai *bhel puri* and *sev puri*.

⑤Tea Centre
Resham Bhawan,
78 Veer Nariman Rd, Churchgate.
Ph: 2281 9142
Daily 8am - 11pm.

An oasis of calm and charm. Established by the Government of India in 1956 to promote sale and consumption of teas. Try the Darjeeling, or explore FTGFOP1, CTCBP, FBOP or just enjoy a simple masala chai. There is a tea bazaar on the side of the restaurant offering a full range of tea accessories – pots, kettles, mugs and even tea cosies!

①Theobroma
Cusrow Baug, Shop 24, Colaba Causeway.
Ph: 2283 0101, 6529 2929, 2287 3778
Daily 11am - 11pm.

This family-run patisserie is seriously delicious. Kainaz was inspired by her mother, Kamal, and left her career at the Oberoi to step out on her own to create Theobroma. Greek for *'food of the gods'*, in this case the name translates to the best desserts and sweets in town.

SNACK

①Kailash Prabat Hindu Hotel (KP's)
Sheela Mahal,
1st Pasta Lane, Colaba.
Ph: 2281 0922
Daily 8am - 11pm.

Famous for their *pani puris* in Karachi, the Mulchandani family opened this restaurant when they moved to Bombay at the time of Partition. There are many KP's throughout the city, but *make the pilgrimage to the original, a landmark for Sindhi food.*

The *puris* are a total taste sensation of crispy, warm sweet and sour. Delicious and designed for eating in one mouthful. Share plates of fresh *pani puris* (Rs.17 for six) in front of the stall, or try the famous Mumbai *bhel puri*. For breakfast, the *dhal pakwan* is great.

Chowpatty Beach

STREET FOOD & SNACKS

Chowpatty at dusk is a carnival and an excellent place to sample Mumbai's delicious street food. Juhu Beach in NoBo is another street food paradise and there are many other Khau Galis *(literally 'eat streets')* scattered throughout the city. Soam, Swati Snacks and Kailash Parbat serve hygenic versions of all of Mumbai's street food. Here are a few street foods not to miss:

Vada Pav

The signature street-side snack and proudly touted as working people's food. Round *pav* buns stuffed with mashed potato and *vadas* (batter fried balls) are served with spicy chutney, made from garlic, coconut and tear-inducing chillies. Other versions include the *Bhaji Pav, Anda Pav* and even a samosa *Pav.*

Bhel Puri

A mix of crushed *puris* (deep fried disks of flour), puffed rice, *sev* (fine chickpea flour crushed crispy noodles), diced onion, boiled potatoes, coriander leaves and green chillies. It is tossed with chutneys: a brown one of a sweet tamarind jaggery, a garlicky red one, and a spicy green chilli one.

Pani Puri

Built around a crisp hollow round puri, stuffed with sprouted *mung* beans, chickpeas and boiled potatoes. It is dunked first in a sweet tamarind chutney and then in ice cold *pani*, a thin watery mint flavoured liquid spiked with chillies. Eaten in one mouthful.

'The Sandwich of Mumbai'

Made from three slices of white bread slathered with butter and spicy coriander chutney, plus sliced potato, cucumber, onion, tomato, cooked beetroot, topped with sauce or ketchup. Sometimes, spicy pea and potato mash is added before the sandwich is toasted.

Masala chai fuels the metropolis. The Mumbai version is a hot, simmered concoction, creamy and fragrant with spices. 'Ek cutting chai! paani kum' loosely translates to 'one half tea with less water'. That's how Mumbaikars order their daily tea. Everyone has their favourite chaiwallah, so choosing one is controversial!

Lassi, served chilled, is traditionally made by blending yogurt, water, salt and ground roasted cumin until it is light and frothy. Sometimes it is sweetened with sugar; a Gujarati version is spiked with fresh coriander and green chillies!

CHAI
⑥ Yadzani Bakery
11/11A Cawasji Patel Street, Fort
(opp Flora Fountain, American Dried Fruit Stores is a good landmark; take laneway winding back. Yadzani is well known and loved, so getting directions is easy.).
Ph: 2287 0739

This small family-run bakery serves a seriously good cup of chai and an excellent *brun maksa. My favourite choice for a cuppa. Try it.*

LASSI
⑤ K Rustom & Co
Stadium House, 87A Veer Nariman Rd, Churchgate (opp Ambassador Hotel).
Phone: 2282 1768
Daily 9.30am - 11pm. Sun 3pm - 11pm.

Do not be put off by the well-worn appearances of this little shop. For 55 years, K Rustom has been serving best lassi in the city. A good place to grab an ice cream and stroll along Marine Drive.

FALOODA
⑪ Badshah
152/156 L T Marg
(opp Crawford Market), Kalbadev.
Ph: 2342 1943, 2344 9316, 2342 5950

The Royal Falooda is the star of the show at this 99-year-old restaurant; the top-secret recipe gives you a sweet pink milk drink served with ice-cream. Very busy, with crowds enjoying these rose fancies and fresh juices and shakes.

CAFES

Moshe's

7, Minoo Manor, Cuffe Parade
(opp the fishing village).
Ph: 2216 1226/1266
Daily 7.30am - midnight.

Located in a stylish converted bungalow, Moshes is a comfortable space serving bistro fare and wines. The bagel breakfast and coffee is popular with local Mumbai yuppies. Additional locations include: Fab India, Kala Ghoda, Golds Gym, Napean Sea Rd and Crosswords Bookstore, Kemps Corner.

By The Way

Pandita Ramabai Rd, Gamdevi, Girgaum
(next to Gamdevi Police Station).
Ph: 2380 3532, 2380 8005
Daily 11am - 11pm.

This café is just around the corner from Mani Bhavan, Gandhi House *(pg13)*. *Run by the Seva Sadan Society, By The Way is dedicated to the empowerment of underprivileged girls and women.* Stop by for a coffee or tea and some home-style food in the modern air-conditioned café and help support a worthy cause.

COFFEE

SOUTH INDIAN COFFEE

Café Mysore

1/461 Durlabh Nivas, Bhau Daji Rd, Matunga (opp B. N. Maheshwari Udyan, right on the King's Circle).
Ph 2402 1230
Daily 6.30am - 10pm. Closed Wed.
Summer hours shortened, call to check.

Proudly declaring itself to be the oldest restaurant in Mumbai for South Indian delicacies, Café Mysore is particularly famed for serving the best filter coffee in town.

We recommend you support organisations that are socially and/ or ennvironmentally sustainable, identified here with the Conscious Travel symbol (pg149)

THE NEW COFFEE CULTURE

Fast taking over the traditional chai culture in the city are the coffee chains popping up on every corner, such as:

Barista

5/4, Grants Bldg,
Arthur Bunder Rd,
Colaba Causeway
(next to Regal Cinema).
Ph 6633 6835
Daily 8.30am - 1.30am.

The premium coffee chain started this branch in 2000. The espressos are good and they serve imported Lavazza coffee. Wi-Fi is available for Rs.113 for two hours.

Café Coffee Day

Marine Drive, Chowpatty.
Daily 8am - midnight.

Founded by a coffee plantation owner, this is the largest chain in India, serving good quality coffee in buzzy environments. The Chowpatty branch has a nice outdoor patio area for soaking up the scene.

COASTAL

④ Trishna

Sai Baba Marg, Kala Ghoda, Fort
(behind Khyber Restaurant, nr Rhythm House).
Ph: 2261 4991, 2270 3213/14/15
Daily noon - 3.30pm, 6.15pm - 12.30am.
Reservation advised.

This is my favourite spot in Mumbai for dinner. All seafood is caught daily by the restaurant's own trawler. Squid koliwada is a must-try, followed by butter pepper garlic crab and Hyderabadi pomfret. Try an Indian wine.

An intimate, historic restaurant, Trishna is also a place for Indian and international celebrities and power-brokers. *Ask to sit in the first room. It feels almost too popular now but, as a complete experience, it is hard to beat.*

THE REST

⑥ Ankur

M P Shetty Marg Fort.
Ph: 2265 4194
Daily noon - 3.30pm, 6pm - 11.30pm.

Ankur is a humble Mangalorean place that looks after its famous clientele well. India's most celebrated chefs come here for the crab in garlic sauce and the semolina coated shrimps.

⑥ Apoorva

Vasta House (Noble Chambers),
S A Brelvi Marg, nr Horniman Circle, Fort.
Ph: 2287 00335
Daily 11.30am - 4pm, 6pm - midnight.

Good prawn *koliwada*, fried fish and *gassi* (gravy) dishes.

⑥ Excellansea

Bharat House, 317 Shahid Bhagat Singh Rd
(opp Fort Market).
Ph: 6635 9945, 2261 8991
Daily 11.30am - 4pm, 5.30pm - midnight.

Famous for South Indian crab and also good for lobster.

Eating ('Night')

MOST EXCLUSIVE

① The Chef's Studio

Taj Mahal Palace & Tower,
Apollo Bunder, Colaba.
Ph: 6665 3366 Ex. 3111
Daily 7pm - 11.45pm.
Reservation essential, book through the Zodiac Grill.

In the mood for the best food in the city and can't decide between Indian, Japanese, French or Chinese, then enjoy the absolute premium experience at the Taj Hotel. This is the personal passion of Hemant Oberoi, Executive Grand Chef.

A table of six people set along side a kitchen island, in an exclusive room, will enjoy the best of the best, presented by the Chefs from Wasabi, Zodiac Grill, Golden Dragon and Masala Art. Make sure to book for when Hemant is in town and enjoy every unforget-table moment. Prices start at Rs.8,000 per person.

② Konkan

Taj President Hotel, Cuffe Parade.
Ph: 6665 0808
Daily 12.30pm - 2.45pm, 7pm - 11.45pm.

Enter Konkan and you are transported
to a Mangalorean village. The food
is a celebration of slow-cooked and
hand-crafted *masalas*. Make sure to
try a coastal *thali*.

⑥ Mahesh Lunch Home

8B Cawasji Patel St, nr Strand Books.
Ph: 2202 3965
Daily noon - 4pm, 6pm - midnight.

The first Mangalorean seafood restaurant
in the city. Much loved, its cuisine sets the bar.
Great crab *masala*, *neer dosa* and prawn *gassi*.

NORTH INDIAN

⑪ Shalimar Restaurant

Shalimar Corner, Vazir Bldg,
Bhendi Bazzar, Bhuleshwar.
Ph: 2345 6630
Daily 8am - 1am.

Foodies from across India come for the
Mughlai food. Shalimar's owners breed their
own livestock and grind their own masalas.
Filled with locals and located in the throng
of the bazaar, Shalimar is welcoming to
the traveller who has been smart enough to
find it. No alcohol is served and this is not
a lingering experience. *The food is authentic,*
delicious and costs a fraction of that at more
touristy Khyber.

⑥ Sher E Punjab

264 Shaheed Bhagat Singh Rd, nr GPO, Fort.
Ph: 2262 1188, 2265 9454
Daily noon - 11.30pm.

Famous for bringing tandoori chicken to
Mumbai, this restaurant opened in 1937 and
offers a full Punjabi food experience. *Terrific.*
The newer restaurant across the road serves
the same food and alcohol.

OTHERS

⑥ Khyber

145 Mahatma Gandhi Rd, Fort.
Ph: 2267 3228
Daily 12.30pm - 4pm,
7.30pm - midnight.

Khyber is the tourist spot
for a high-end Indian meal.
The huge multi-roomed
restaurant has some
wonderful Indian art on
display. The food is abundant
and the service attentive.

③ Kandahar

At the Oberoi for traditonal
Indian in lavish style.

① Masala Kraft

At the Taj Mahal Palace
Hotel for contemporary
Indian. A good five-star
experience.

OLD BOMBAY

⑤ The Society

The Ambassador Hotel,
Veer Nariman Rd, Churchgate.
Ph: 2204 1131

A *'fine dining'* experience little changed from when the restaurant began in 1949. Society is a little more subdued now than it was in its glamorous heyday, but the mirrors, marble and gilt remain. The pianist still performs nightly – you will find charming music request cards on each table. The cuisine also takes you back in time, fondue savoyarde or chateaubriand anyone? *Love it or loathe it, this will not be to everyone's taste. Quirky, but a gem.*

⑥ Gaylord

Mayfair, Veer Nariman Rd,
Mayfair, Churchgate.
Ph: 2204 4693
Daily 12.30pm - 3.30pm,
7.30pm - 11.30pm.
The terrace is open from 9.30am serving breakfast, snacks and a very nice afternoon tea. The bakery is open all day.

Gaylord is a 50-year-old Bombay institution serving reliable Indian food and timeless continental fare. The lush terrace is a good place to drop into for a restorative cuppa and something delightful from the bakery.

SEXIEST

① Indigo

4 Mandlik Rd, off Colaba Causeway,
behind Taj Mahal Hotel.
Ph: 6636 8999
Daily noon - 3pm, 7.30pm - midnight.
(Reservations essential,
two dinner seatings 8pm - 10pm).

Even after seven years Indigo is still the hottest spot in town. *This is the Mumbai scene.* Dress up, look hip, feel sexy. Enjoy one of the best wine lists in town, good Mediterranean food and polished service.

⑧ Salt Water Grill

H20 Water Sports Complex, next to Mafatlal
Swimming Club, Chowpatty, Marine Drive.
Ph: 2368 5485
Daily 4.30pm - 7pm for sunset snacks. Dinner
served 7.30pm - midnight. Bookings advised.

Mumbai's sexiest restaurant, this is Goa relocated to the Chowpatty beach. Super-sylish and relaxed, hammocks, loungers and dining canopies lie on white sand under the palm trees. *The ambience is better than the food.* A perfect place to enjoy drinks and light snacks. Also good for brunch on the weekends.

INTERNATIONAL:

ITALIAN

③ Vetro

The Oberoi Hotel, Nariman Point.
Ph: 6632 5757
Daily 12.30pm - 2.45pm, 7.30pm - 11.30pm.

A stunning space with a wonderful use of coloured and clear glass. The walk-in antipasto room forms a great beginning to a fine meal; the Enoteca Wine Library stores over 900 bottles.

FRENCH

❶ Zodiac

Taj Mahal Palace & Tower, Apollo Bunder, Colaba.
Ph: 6665 3366
Daily 12.30pm - 2.45pm, 7pm - 11.45pm.
Closed Sun Lunch.

This is a grand, grown-up restaurant for old-fashioned romance. You are cocooned from the world, under a domed ceiling with twinkling stars with lovely golden light. The piano player and the über-professional staff make the evening glide. Those who find it stuffy and pricey may be missing the point: *this is not for the hip, the trendy or the super cool – it is a classic.*

The Camembert dariole soufflé is the signature dish, and classics such as chateaubriand join the best ingredients from around the world, including truffles, caviar and foie gras. *The wine list is the best in town.*

ASIAN

❸ Vongwong

Express Towers, First Floor
(entrance from Ramnath Goenka Marg),
Nariman Point (behind the Air India bldg).
Phone 2287 5633/34/35
Daily 12.30pm - 3pm, 7.30pm - 12.30am.

The stylish décor is a backdrop to some of the best Asian food in India. Named after two master chefs, the Vong menu is Thai and the Wong, Chinese.

Of the 300 dishes available, do try the Chilean seabass, the egg curry and the tom yum soup. From a window seat you can watch Mumbai taxis whizz past – it is nice to see a restaurant that has not shut itself off from the city.

CHINESE

❻ Royal China

Behind Sterling Cinema,
Hazarimal Somani Marg, Fort.
Ph: 6635 5310/1
Daily noon - 3pm,
7pm - midnight.

A sophisticated softly-lit restaurant serving seriously good food. The crispy aromatic duck is acclaimed and the special menus are a good way to savour the experience. The lunchtime dim sum menu is the best in the city.

❿ CG83

123 A K Marg, Om Chambers,
Kemps Corner.
Ph: 2363 0841/2353 5588
Daily 12.30pm - 2.45pm,
7.30pm - 11.45pm.
Reservations recommended.

Nelson Wang is the father of Indian Chinese food and is one of the country's most beloved chefs. Adding the Indian flair, he created famous Manchurian chicken, now served in restaurants and street carts across the country. The recently opened CG83 is luxuriously decorated, hugely popular and serves a wide range of Nelson's signature food. *Make sure to have the pepper chilli prawns.*

THAI

② Thai Pavilion

Taj President Hotel,
Cuffe Parade.
Ph: 6665 0808
Daily 12.30pm - 3.00pm,
7.30pm - 11.45pm.

The first exclusive Thai
restaurant in India and
arguably still the best.
Recently reopened with a
glamorous contemporary
look and foodies are raving
about the total experience.
Adjacent is the hip **Wink
Bar**, perfect for an after-
dinner drink.

JAPANESE

① Wasabi

Taj Mahal Palace & Tower,
Apollo Bunder, Colaba.
Ph: 6665 3366
Daily 12.30pm - 2.45pm,
7pm - 11.45pm. Closed Sun
lunch. Reservations, at least
two days in advance, are
essential.

Mumbai's most expensive
restaurant serves the finest
sushi in town. Master
Chef Masaharu Morimoto
uses authentic Japanese
ingredients and techniques
to present the best
contemporary Japanese food
in India. Set lunch menus
offer good value; the tatami
room features private dinners
with traditonal service. *Condé
Nast included this in their Best
100 Restaurants in the World.*

DESSERT

⑪ Taj Ice Cream

36/40 Sayed Abu Mohammed Rd, Bohri Mohalla
(Khara Tank Rd), Bhendi Bazzaar, Bhuleshwar.
Ph: 2346 1257 & Hatim's mobile is 98206 35292.
Daily 9am - midnight.

Abbasbhai Icecreamwalla (real name!) is the
fourth generation of the Icecreamwalla family
and oversees the 110-year-old business still
serving ice cream in the same place with the
same recipe. The secret to the taste lies in the
hand-made method of churning the cream
using a big iron rod, called the *sancha*. *The best
ice cream I have ever had. Look out Berthillion!*

⑧ New Kulfi Centre

Marina Mansion, S.V.P. Rd, Chowpatty Junction.
Ph: 2368 4291, 2368 9059
Daily 10.30am - 1am.

Watch your kulfi being sliced, weighed on
jewellers' scales and served on a fresh green leaf.
Famous for its NKC Special.

LATE NIGHT

⑧ Bachelor's Juice House

Marine Drive, nr Chowpatty.
Ph: 2368 1408
Daily 11am - 1.30am or later!

*A Mumbai institution, this simple roadside stall has
served seasonal fruits, ice-cream and milkshakes to your
car since 1945.* Famous in winter for strawberries
and cream; pre-monsoon try the fresh mango
with ice cream. Popular with kissing couples.

① Bademiya

Tulloch Rd, Apollo Bunder
(in a shabby laneway directly behind
Taj Mahal Palace Hotel).
Phone 2284 8038, 2285 1649
Daily 7.30pm - 4am!

For the last 50 years, crowds have been
gathering every night for kebabs around
this open-air charcoal grill. There are over
40 options of *kebab roti* rolls and now there are
even some vegetarian choices. Eat on the street
or take-away. *Only for those with a strong constitution
or who are fearless. Locals love it.*

Drinking

BARS

⑤The Dome

Intercontinental Hotel, 135 Marine Drive.
Ph: 3987 9999
Daily 6pm - 12.30am.

This is the finest bar in Mumbai to watch the sun set over the Arabian Sea and to see the lights of Marine Drive become the queen's necklace. A chic bar with a chilled soundtrack, excellent drinks and sophisticated snacking. A terrific saxophonist, Woody, plays Tuesdays through Thursdays.

①Royal Bombay Yacht Club

Chatarapati Shivaji Maharaj Marg,
Apollo Bunder, nr the Gateway of India.
Ph: 2202 1880

The most historic character-filled bar in the city. Get invited by a member or see if your club had reciprocal rights with this loved institution. *A national treasure.*

①Leopold Café

Colaba Causeway, Colaba.
Ph: 2202 0131, 2287 3362
Daily 8am - midnight.

An institution on the Colaba scene since 1871. Gregory David Roberts, the author of *Shantaram,* still frequents the bar and may be cajoled into signing a book. Copies on sale at Leopold. The buzzy vibe begins at breakfast and hums along until late night. Ideal for a few *'cleansing ales'* (aka beers)!

①Café Mondegar

Metro House, 5 Colaba Causeway.
Ph 2202 0591
Daily 8am - 12.30am.

Café by day, happening bar by night. The mural by Goan cartoonist Mario Miranda adds charm. Its cold, cheap pitchers of beer are popular with both foreigners and locals.

⑯The Tasting Room

Good Earth Shop,
Raghuvanshu Mills, Senapati
Bapat Marg, Lower Parel
Ph: 2495 1954, 2495 3840

The Sula-owned wine bar is closed at time of writing due to some government licensing issues. They are hoping to reopen.

①Tendulkars

1st Floor, Narang House,
34 Chatrapati Shivaj Marg,
between the Regal Cinema &
the Gateway of India, Colaba.
Ph: 2282 9934
Daily noon - 3pm,
7.30pm - midnight.

This resto-bar is owned by Mumbai's famous cricketer and full of cricket memorabilia and has big TV screens. When a match is on, it is likely you will find both teams partying here.

⑰Jewel of India

Nehru Centre, Dr. Annie
Besant Rd, Worli.

Ph: 2494 9435/204/214
/217/219
Daily 12.30pm - 3pm,
7pm - 11.30pm.

THE power bar in this part of town. Frequented by advertising *'suits'* and businessmen drinking whisky. The restaurant is also popular but I have never made it after liberal free snacks at happy-hour (6.30pm - 8pm).

RESTAURANT BARS

①Indigo

4 Mandlik Rd, off Colaba
Causeway,
behind Taj Mahal Hotel.
Ph: 6636 8999
Daily noon - 3pm,
7.30pm - midnight.

The two bars at Indigo, the
ground-floor and the roof-
top-bar are the place to see
the glitterati in full force.
An excellently stocked bar
with a very good wine list,
including by the glass.

①Tetsuma

41/44 Dr Minoo Desai Marg,
nr Privé, behind Radio Club.
Ph: 2287 6578
Daily 12.30pm-3pm, 7.30pm-
11.30pm.

Designer Japanese/Asian
bar and restaurant. A
sophisticated oasis of calm.
Perfect for drinks and
tempura snacks, or a full
dinner. On Monday evenings
enjoy the Chefs Banquet,
where you can choose
anything (or everything!)
from the sushi, sashimi and à
la carte menu, for Rs.1,300
plus tax per person. The
lunch time special is also
good value, with unlimited
sushi and sashimi for
Rs.800 plus tax (not
available on Sunday).

①Henry Tham

Dhanraj Mahal Apollo Bunder.
Ph: 2202 3186, 2284 8214
Daily 12.30pm - 3.30pm, 7.30pm - midnight.

The stylish modern Asian restaurant opened to
much gourmet acclaim a few years ago and is
now more famous for its swanky lounge. This is
one of the hottest places to party in the city and
has live music at the weekends.

BEST FUN

⑤Not Just Jazz by the Bay

Soona Mahal, 143 Marine Drive.
Ph: 2282 0957, 2285 1876, 2282 0833
Daily noon - 3pm, 6pm - 2am.

A happening spot in Mumbai for the last
decade. Regular clientele have brass nameplates
at the bar. Live bands Wed through Sat, karaoke
Sun through Tues. Cover charges apply.

NIGHTLIFE

⑰Shiro

Bombay Dyeing Mill Compound,
Pandurang Budhkar Marg
(opp Kamala Mills Film Studio), Worli.
Ph: 2438 3008
Daily 7.30pm - 1.30am.

Mumbai's answer to New York's Tao or Paris's
Buddha Bar. *'Shiro' means castle in Japanese* and
this hip space features towering ceilings
and dramatic décor. Good cocktails and
Asian fusion food.

①Privé

41/44 Mon repos,
Ground Floor,
Minoo Desai Rd, Colaba.
Ph: 2202 8700

The most upscale private members' club in
Mumbai. However, out of town visitors will
be welcomed with advance arrangement
by concierges at good hotels. Owned by the
Chateau Indage group, it serves an extensive
range of wines and spirits. Bottles of Dom
Perignon are served with sparklers and music!

IIb DELICIOUS
NoBo Dining:

Until the 1970s, Bombay meant SoBo. But as the city spread north, the beach shacks on Juhu beach were transformed into some of the city's finest homes and hotels.

Bollywood, the IT industry and a full range of commercial enterprises all made their bases in the north.

As a result, many SoBo restaurants created a second outlet north. Many are now adding a third outlet as the city (and the traffic) continues to expand.

SoBo Dining: (pg17)

The selection in these pages is a highly-edited list of the places special to Mumbai.

Note: the 'Day' and 'Night' descriptors are subjective categorisations, as most places offer all-day service!

Eating ('Day')

BEST LOVED

Prithvi Café

Prithvi Theatre,
Janki Kutir Society, Juhu Tara Rd.
Ph: 2617 4118
Mon 3pm-11.30pm.
Tues to Sun, 12.30pm-11.30pm.

A bohemian outdoor café located at the theatre Mecca of Mumbai. This intimate café is hugged by trees and is patronised by an arty crowd. A regular haunt for actors and directors talking scripts and deals. Make sure to have the legendary Irish coffee.

BEST EATING ADVENTURE

Govinda

ISKCON Hare Krishna Land,
nr Juhu Church, Juhu Rd.
Ph: 2620 0337, 2620 6860
Daily 7.30am-10.30pm.

We recommend you support organisations that are socially and/ or environmentally sustainable, identified here with the Conscious Travel symbol (pg149)

Chant, be happy, and get very well fed! Visitors are welcomed and there is no pressure to be a devotee at this temple located in a calm leafy area of Juhu. Walk past the temple area and accommodation block to enter into a huge, glistening dining hall. Colourful table-settings are adorned with fresh roses; piped *bhanjans* (sacred hymns) provide a calm air.

The pure vegetarian food (both Indian and Western) is delicious, and there are good fresh juices. Occasionally the hall is booked for a wedding so it is worth calling to check. Govinda serves breakfast at 7.30am, lunch from 12.30pm, snacks from 4pm and a dinner from 7.30pm.

BREAKFAST

POWER BREAKFAST

25 Lotus Café

J W Marriott Hotel, Juhu Tara Rd.
Ph: 6693 3276
Daily 24 hours.

This grand open space at the base of a sweeping staircase provides North Mumbai's most lavish breakfast, as well as fabulous views of the lotus pond and out to the ocean. The buffet breakfast is a lavish affair and the hugely popular Sunday brunch has live jazz.

In Bandra the power breakfast is at **Vista**, at the Taj Lands End Hotel *(pg144)*.

COMFORT BREAKFAST

21 The Bagel Shop

Below Barefoot, Pali Mala Rd,
off Carter Rd, Bandra (W).
Ph: 2605 0178
Daily 9am - 10pm.

This is a relaxed neighbourhood drop-in-spot in a charming location, nestled between boutiques in one of Bandra's small leafy lanes. Sit on the comfy furniture and enjoy a small menu of simple food and fresh juices.

LUNCH

Virtually all of the entries in the *'Night'* section are open for lunch. Olive *(pg39)* is particularly good. *One place I think is best at lunch is the following:*

SOUTH INDIAN

25 Woodlands Garden Café

Juhu Scheme, VM Rd, Vile Parle (W).
Ph: 2611 9119
Daily noon - 11pm.

An authentic and much-loved no-frills place. Take to the sprawling roof-top terrace, or sit in air-conditioned comfort in the restaurant to snack on *dosas* or South Indian *thali*.

CAFES

Bandra has a huge range of bustling cafés. Some favourites include the following:

22 Crêpe Station

www.crepestationcafe.com
8-9 Gagangiri Apts
(off Carter Rd,
Union Park, Khar).
Ph: 2648 5482, 3260 6448
Daily 8am - midnight.

India's first crêperie started in 2003 as two tables and a few benches. It has since grown in size and expanded to a Juhu branch with plans for 25 more outlets. This laid-back seaside location is an all-day café that serves good breakfasts and the best beef burger in town.

Other branch:

25 3-4 Ashiana Apts.
next to Arogaya Nidhi
Hospital, 13th NS Rd, Juhu.
Ph: 2670 5208

21 Café Coffee Day

Gagangiri Commercial
Complex on Carter Rd,
Bandra.
Daily 9am - 1.30am.

Great views of Arabian Sea, and a good open-air deck.

21 Café Basilicio

St Johns Rd, next to HDFC
Bank, Pali Naka, Bandra.
Daily 7.30am - 12.30am.

A stylish central spot. The courtyard is pretty but noisy.

Eating ('Night')

COASTAL DINNER

23 Mahesh Lunch Home (MLH)

Nr JW Marriot, Juhu Tara Rd,
Santacruz (W).
Ph: 6695 5559
Daily noon - 3.30pm,
7pm - 12.30am.

MLH is my personal favourite for dinner in Mumbai. The original MLH at Fort in South Mumbai was the first Mangalorean restaurant, but this northern branch is bigger, brighter and busier. Enjoy fabulous coastal food. Prawn *gassi* with *neer dosa* especially recommended.

24 Spice Tree

Fernandez Villa, 95 Hill Rd,
Bandra (W).
Ph: 2640 5053
Daily noon - 3.30pm,
7pm - midnight.

A stylish local, serving a very good coastal menu. Ask to sit under the wooden rafters in the Cinnamon Room or beyond the bar into the intimate Cardamon Room. Try dining alfresco on the Clove Terrace.

Elco

SNACKS & STREET FOOD

24 Elco

2/A Elco Market, 46 Hill Rd, Bandra (W).
Ph: 2645 7677, 2643 7206
Daily 9.30am - 11.30pm. Sun 6am - noon.

Opened as a street stall in 1970, Elco is now run by the founder's sons as a multi-level, air-conditioned restaurant. I recommend staying outside with the crowds at the hugely popular stalls to taste the best *pani puri* and Mumbai *chaats*. It is impossible to spend more than Rs.100. Stars and street kids mingle happily.

25 Juhu Beach

This is the Chowpatty of the North. At sunset, it becomes a bustling scene of *chaatwallahs* serving the famous *bhel puri* and other snacks to the hungry local crowds.

NORTH INDIAN

Peshawari and Dum Pukht

ITC Grand Maratha Sheraton & Towers
Sahar Rd, Andheri.
Ph: 2830 3030
Daily 12.30pm-2.45pm, 7pm-11.45pm.
Reservations essential.

The Times' Food Guide dubs *Peshawari*
'a carnivore's Mecca'. This foodie destination
serves rugged northwest cuisine in a rustic
setting. Often described as the equivalent
to Bukhara in Delhi, this is a finger-eating,
bib-wearing place and has robust fare.
You can now take home cans of the famous
dal, which is simmered all night.

Dum Pukht is a more sophisticated gourmet
favourite with slow-cooked North Indian
cuisine. The décor is refined and luxurious.

SOUTH INDIAN

Dakshin

ITC Grand Maratha Sheraton & Towers
Sahar Rd, Andheri.
Ph: 2830 3030
Daily 12.30pm-2.45pm, 7pm-11.45pm.
Reservations essential.

This good-looking restaurant is also part of
the *'Gourmet Hotel'* and is the most up-scale
South Indian restaurant in the city. Ornate
décor and excellent food.

SEXIEST

Seijou and the Soul Dish

Krystal, 2nd floor, 206, Waterfield Rd,
Patkar Marg, Bandra (W).
(above ICICI Bank, opp Stomach Restaurant).
Ph: 2640 1193
Daily 7.30pm-1am.

Sexy, sophisticated and stunning. This 10,000
sq.ft. restaurant is seductively designed with
great lighting, abundant candles and then
an open-air roof to gaze at the stars. Serves
pan-Asian food and good cocktails.

Olive Bar and Kitchen

Pali Hill Tourist Hotel,
14 Union Park, Bandra.
Ph: 2605 8228, 2605 8229
Daily 12.30pm-3.30pm,
7.30pm-1.30am.

*Established in 2000, Olive is
an institution.* The whitewashed, candle-lit restaurant
and bar are always buzzing
with beautiful people
relaxing in the sexy indoor/
outdoor space enjoying
Mediterranean food. The
flea market and the gourmet
market evenings are held
monthly. The clientele is
clad in stilettos and jeans,
not a sari or a kurta in
sight. You can almost forget
you are in India, however
Chef Max has a true
passion for India and is
now cooking foie gras in the
Tandoor.

Aurus

Nichani Kutir, Ground Floor
Nichani House, Juhu Tara Rd,
Santa Cruz
(enter from the laneway next
to Anita Dongre Showroom).
Ph: 6710 6666/67
Daily 8.30pm-1.30am.

*This newcomer on the Juhu
Scene is completely sexy.* The
candlelit deck on the edge
of the beach is one of the
best spots in all of Mumbai.

The indoor restaurant is
more formal and elegant.
Come for the view and
the vibe and drink in the
glamorous scene. Excellent
cocktails and a well-stocked
bar, though average service
and unremarkable interna-
tional cuisine.

Drinking

BARS

ITALIAN

②Don Giovanni
www.dongiovanniristorante.com

Hotel Bawa Continental,
Juhu Tara Rd, Juhu.
Ph: 2615 3125
Daily 11.30am-3pm,
6.30pm-11.30pm.

A romantic old-fashioned restaurant, Don Giovanni is intimate and grown up (no children allowed!). Created by Giovanni Federico who missed home-style Italian food, it is now regarded as the unofficial Italian Embassy of Mumbai. Giovanni is enthusiastic in assisting you with the menu. Make sure to try the *ravioli di magro* and enjoy the excellent selection of Italian wines.

BEST SUNSET

②Vie Sunset
Lounge & Deck
www.vie.co.in

102 Juhu Tara Rd,
Santa Cruz (W).
(opp Little Italy).
Ph: 2660 3003
Daily 7pm-1.30am.
Breakfast Sun 8am-11am.

Fabulous. The outside deck is superb – you feel you are almost touching the sea. Sip a cocktail or a fine wine and enjoy a vista of the whole beach. There is also great people watching and spectacular sunsets. Often booked for private parties, so call ahead.

②Aqua Spirit
Sun'n'Sand Hotel, 39 Juhu Beach.
Ph: 6693 8888
Daily 11.30am-3pm, 6.30pm until late.

This bar replaced the much-loved Beachcomber Bar popular with the Bollywood crowd since the 60s. While the old character may be gone, this contemporary lounge space is stylish and has a great happy hour until 7.30pm. The outside bar is a good place to watch the sunset over the beach with a beer. Then, eat at the adjoining restaurant, the ever-popular Kebab Hut.

②Toto's Garage
30 Lourdes Heaven, Pali Junction, Bandra.
Ph: 2600 5494
Daily 6pm -1.30am.

A Bandra institution, this small, smoky bar plays loud rock'n'roll to a buoyant crowd. A VW Beetle hangs over the bar. A great kick-start to a bar crawl.

②Hawaiian Shack
339, 16th Rd, opp Mini Punjab, Bandra (W).
Ph: 2605 8753
Daily 7pm -1.30am.

A Bandra bar crawl must. Mood lighting and pop and retro music entertain a happy crowd drinking cocktails and beers. Drinks lack frilly umbrellas but the staff are in Hawaiian shirts.

BEST FUN

②Soul Fry
Silver Craft, Pali Mala Rd, opp Pali Market, Bandra.
Ph: 2604 6892
Daily 12.30pm-2.30pm, 7.30pm-12.30am.

Karaoke nights have this place hopping on a Mon, so go early and grab a table to enjoy fabulous home-style Goan seafood, cold beer and a lot of fun. All week this beloved little place is happily buzzing, often with jazz or live bands. Excellent food makes this the best dining stop on a bar crawl. Good lunchtime seafood *thali* too.

NIGHTLIFE

Zenzi
www.zenzi-india.com

183 Waterfield Rd, Bandra (W).
Ph: 6643 0670
Daily 11.30am - 1.30am.

A 7,000 sq.ft. international lounge bar and restaurant. Popular with local Bandra yuppies and expats; good for looking at the Bandra scene. Features fusion food, live music, comedy and salsa dancing.

Enigma
J.W.Marriott, Juhu Tara Rd, Juhu.
Ph: 6693 3000
Tues to Sat 10pm - 3am.

Best club in Mumbai – A-list celebs and stars party hard and late; busiest Friday, Saturday.

Poison
Krystal, 206, Waterfield Rd, Patkar Marg, Bandra (W). Beneath Seijou Restaurant, behind ICIC Bank.
Ph: 2642 3006
Daily 9.30pm - 1.30am.

Big, high energy, brash and loud. A steady stream of Bollywood celebs can be seen coming and going from VIP members' area.

At the Airport

DOMESTIC AIRPORT

The closest hotel is the *Orchid (pg146)*. The roof top bar and restaurant, *Mostly Grills*, which overlooks the runway, is an interesting spot for a drink along side the hotel pool. There is also a 24-hour coffee shop and a bar, open 9am until midnight.

The Grand Hyatt (pg146) is about 20 mins from the airport depending upon traffic. It has five specialty restaurants (open plan and off the main lobby); Italian, Chinese, Indian, a grill and a 24-hour café. *The Gourmet Store* is open daily from 7am - 10pm. Set up as the deli for the residential apartments, it has the best sandwiches in Mumbai. Choose fresh bagels or baguettes, excellent cold-cuts, cheeses and great fresh salads and good Illy coffee.

INTERNATIONAL AIRPORT

ITC, Grand Maratha Sheraton & Towers (pg147) has the best selection of dining including the famed North Indian restaurants *Peshawari* and *Dum Pukht (pg39)* and the South Indian restaurant *Dakshin (pg39)*.

Le Royal Meridien (pg146) is a stylish and sexy choice. The lobby lounge has a shimmering Austrian crystal chandelier. The luxurious lounge bar is open until 2am and has a walk-in humidor. There is a 24-hour brasserie and a good Chinese restaurant with stylish décor, open until midnight.

The Hyatt Regency (pg147) has a good 24-hour buffet. The bar opens at 5pm and closes at 2am. The Italian restaurant, *Stax*, has an Italian chef and a good reputation.

The Leela (pg147) has a popular lounge and a nice outdoor café next to the pool.

Must-Have's

Bangles and Bindis
from Vividha, Chandra Lok, excellent
for dressing up *(pg67)*.

Bombay Street Pack.
The *'must-have'* arrival set of stylish cotton shirts
and pants for men from Bombay Electric *(pg54)*.

Ganesh Terracotta and sterling silver minature
Ganesh from Frazer & Haws *(pg46)*.

Kolhapuri Chappals
made from soft leather in a rainbow of colours,
from Joy Shoes or Corner Footwear stall on the
Colaba Causeway *(pg63)*.

Mantra Matchboxes and Cheerharan Toilet Paper
from Design Temple *(pg46)*.

Musical instruments.
The Gungroo and Dumroo from Furtado, Mumbai's
much-loved 140-year-old music store *(pg77)*.

Organic Masala Chai Mix
from Conscious Foods warehouse *(pg78)*
or Indigo Deli *(pg21)*.

Shantaram,
the best-selling novel set in Mumbai. Pick it up at
Leopold Café where author, Gregory David Roberts,
is still a regular *(pg33)*.

Sula Dindoori Red Wine.
Mahrashtra's best wine, made from grapes grown
in the Dindoori vineyards, north of Mumbai. From
Shah Wines *(pg78)*.

Vintage Indian Bazaar Treasures
from India's hippest and sexiest lifestyle shop,
Bungalow Eight *(pg45)*.

III FABULOUS

Shopping: Hunting & Gathering

Mumbai is India's commercial hub and it is also the shopping capital of the country.

Here is the definitive shopping guide to ensure you find the best of the local treasures.

Your Portrait

The oldest portrait in the world dates back 27,000 years and was discovered in 2006 at the Vilhonneur grotto near Angoulême.

The world's most famous portrait is Leonardo da Vinci's Mona Lisa.

In Mumbai, pick up a painted portrait, Bollywood style, and a classic photographic portrait.

Best Souvenir

⑱ Balkrishna Art

Matoshri Height D 1 Vaidya Rd, Dadar (W)
(call when close, they will meet you on the main road and guide you).
Ph: 2430 1973 Mobile: 98676 37638
Mon to Sat (Call for an appointment).

Uojwal is now running his fathers business, painting Bollywood posters and outdoor billboards. Bring along your favourite Bollywood poster (DVD/CD) and get a hand-painted version. Even better, bring a favourite photo (preferably a lovers' clinch) and have it painted into the scene Bollywood style. *Uojwal believes bigger is better, so his large pieces would be perfect for a Manhattan loft.* Prices vary on design and size, however an indicative range is Rs.15,000 to Rs.40,000 and shipping can be easily arranged.

⑥ Hamilton Studios

NTC House, Narottam Morarjee Marg.
Ballard Estate.
Ph: 2262 0485, 2261 4544
Mon to Sat, 9am - 1pm, 2pm - 6pm.
Appointment essential.
(Ranjit works between 1pm - 4pm).

Hamilton studios was founded in 1928 and is the oldest operational studio in the city. Mr Ranjit Madhavji fell in love with photography in 1957 and has been running this studio personally for the last 50 years. He describes himself as a very slow person and believes in taking only one shot, so this may take an hour or longer! *His perfectionist nature is that of an artist and his pictures are like paintings.* You will be in good company; Ranjit has photographed gurus, judges, lords and ladies. *A truly wonderful experience.*

Gifts & Great Things

LIFESTYLE

⑤ **Bungalow 8**

www.bungaloweight.com

Wankhede Stadium, North Stand,
E-F Block, D Rd, Churchgate.
Ph: 2281 9880, 2281 9881
Daily 10.30am - 7.30pm.

*An unconventional location is just one of the unique
things about Bungalow 8.* Owner Maithili
Ahluwalia has created one of India's best
shopping experiences. The eclectic collection of homewares, jewellery and fashion is
hand-picked from India and South East Asia
and has touches from around the world, such
as the South African Beauty products.

Bijoy Jain, one of India's leading architects,
designed the 4,000 sq. ft. store. The exposed
concrete space is nestled under the benches
of the stadium. Envisaged as an avant-garde
home, contemporary products are displayed
on vintage furniture pieces. *A must-shop
destination.*

① **Moon River**

1, The Courtyard, SP Centre,
41/44 Minoo Desai Marg, Colaba.
Ph: 6638 5460
Daily 10.30am - 7.30pm.

*A chic shop full of elegant European and Indian
homeware designers,* mainly specialising in glass,
ranging from the seriously sophisticated to fun
and frothy, like the polka dotted espresso cups.
Indian designers include the lovely Devi Design,
who make candle stands in brass and use the
traditional Indian motif of the lotus in different
forms and materials such as copper and silver.
There is an increasing emphasis on Indian craft
forms alongside hand-selected design objects
from around the world. Owner Radhika Gupta
is a Delhi-based jewellery designer and has
curated a selection of beautiful objects for both
the Delhi and Mumbai stores.

*Mumbai has some of
the hottest retail stores
in the world. Enjoy
this selection of the
best on offer.*

*Lifestyle stores help
create a dream of
how we want to live.*

*The good ones have
an inspired collection
of beautiful things
that have you simply
wanting to move in.
The selection here
includes some of the
best in Mumbai...*

LIFESTYLE
(CONT'D)

2 Frazer & Haws

Landmark Bldg, off Turner Rd,
Pali Naka, Bandra (W).
Ph: 6675 0200, 6675 0877
Mon to Sat 10am - 8pm.

Frazer and Haws, founded in 1869 in London, makes exquisite silver collectibles and jewellery.

A manufacturing unit in India was established a decade ago and now houses over 200 craftspeople who are all sixth- and seventh-generation silversmiths and goldsmiths.

The signature packaging alone is enough to spark a major shopping spree. Choose from jewellery or homewares in classic or contemporary English designs and designs inspired by Indian traditions.

The miniature (2 inch) terracotta Ganesh with a touch of sterling silver is a favourite.

1 Design Temple

www.designtemplestore.com

Founded by Divya Thakur in 1999, Design Temple is a Mumbai-based graphic design studio with both a national and international client base.

Divya identified the need for a new Indian design language, one that was modern, mature and stereotypically kitsch. In 2006 Divya and her team brought out their own range of vibrant everyday products based on this thinking.

Edition One includes the Parrot Diaries, Shunya Bags, Holy Smoke Incense Sticks, Mantra Matchboxes (featuring messages for ideal living: safe sex, non violence and saving fuel) and the hugely popular Cheerharan toilet paper. The latter is humorously based on an Indian epic, where the evil Dushasana ordered the stripping of a sari from the noble woman Draupadi, but which never ended as god Krishna gave her his protection.

Edition Two expands upon the core collection by adding stationery and lighting.

Also available at:

Good Earth (pg47), ***Indigo Deli (pg21)*** and ***Barefoot (pg57)***.

⑯Good Earth
www.goodearthindia.com

Raghuvanshi Mansion, Raghuvanshi Mills,
Senapati Bapat Marg, Lower Parel.
Ph: 2495 1954, 2495 3840
Daily 11am - 8pm.

Anita Lal, a designer and potter, established
Good Earth in 1996 to create stylish and
functional products for the home and the
garden, using craft skills and natural materials. Today, Good Earth has expanded to an
impressive mill space and has become one of
the hottest lifestyle destinations in the city.

It has a contemporary Indian aesthetic and
carries an extensive range of exclusively
designed products for dining, entertaining,
and home décor. An excellent place for
gift shopping.

Designers Krsna Mehta and Sangita Jindal
have translated Mumbai icons and the city's
buzzy energy into tangible forms. They
created the Bombay Project, exclusively for
Good Earth.

The dabbawallah finds a place on a mug, the
bhajiyawallah on an art canvas and sari-clad
women juxtaposed with red lipsticks are on
handbags and cushions. This hip collection
contrasts the grand old city with the modern
vibrant city. *Quirky and fun.*

Other branch:

㉕R/154, Juhu Tara Road, Juhu
(opp J.W. Marriot Hotel)
Ph: 2611 2481, 6451 2301.

①Ravissant
www.cest-ravissant.com

New India Centre,
17A Cooperage Rd.
Ph: 2287 3405
Mon to Sat 10am - 7.30pm.

Ravissant, launched in India in
1981, is striving to be India's
first worldwide luxury brand.
Their portfolio includes
fashion, home soft furnishings, silver and jewellery.
They also have two luxury
beauty salons.

Ravissant is founded on
Indian traditional craft and
overlays this with contemporary international designs.
Everything is handcrafted
from fashion to home
furnishing, sterling silver
to jewellery. The jewellery
workshop alone has over
250 Indian master silver
and goldsmiths and some of
them have visited Europe
to teach the technique
of silversmithing, making
Ravissant one of the world's
most reputed manufacturers
of sterling silverware.

Other branches:

①Taj Mahal Hotel,
Lobby Level, Apollo Bunder.

⑩Ravissant, Abhay
Chambers, Kemps Corner.

②Ravissant Store & Salon,
Taj Lands End, Lobby Level,
Bandstand, Bandra (W).

LOCAL CRAFT

⑩ Contemporary Arts & Crafts
www.cac.co.in

19 Napean Sea Rd
(just down from Kemps Cnr).
Ph: 2363 1979
Mon to Sat 10am - 7pm.
Sun 11am - 6.30pm.

Established in 1962, this was the first home store in India to bring east and west together and stocks only goods made in India. CA&C works with a number of NGOs to provide a platform for indigenous Indian arts and crafts, thereby creating a source of income and employment for hundreds of artisans and craftsmen.

Make sure to pick up something from the Auroville-based Maroma range of aromatic products (including 55 varieties of incense). Always on the list to take visitors to – *a friendly store, good for trinkets and gifts.*

㉒ Dhoop
www.dhoopcrafts.com

101 Khar Sheetal Apartments,
Dr Ambedkar Rd, Union Park, Khar (W).
Ph: 2649 8646, 2649 8647, 6581 9351, 6581 9352
Mon to Sat 11am - 8.15pm.

Aradhana Nagpal's passion for craft began as a child attending a craft mela (fair) with her mother. Now, with an MA in Ancient Indian Culture, she works on publishing projects related to the field and in 2003 opened Dhoop. An evening conversation with friends resulted in the name. Aradhana explains it as *'something Indian, something simple and something that is essential to every craft… Dhoop – Sunshine'.*

Dhoop works with not-for-profit organisations and designers that partner with various artisan groups to support the craft skills of India like weaving, bamboo craft, cane, wood carving, hand-painting, pottery, incense-making, embroidery, crochet and patchwork.

The constant need to innovate, design and experiment resulted in Dhoop's in-house research project focusing on natural materials and combining these with various craft skills e.g. a traditional painter to paint on hand-woven banana fabric.

A sunny store, offering home accessories and wearables in contemporary designs. Everything in the store is hand-made by craftspeople from all parts of India, with a special focus on the northeast and the south. Dhoop also hosts an interesting series of events.

NGOs & TRUSTS

⑩ Shraddha Charitable Trust

14-19 Mahalaxmi Municipal School Bldg,
3rd floor, B. Desai Rd
(nr the Mahalaxmi Temple) Kemps Corner.
Ph: 2351 3735, 2352 4463, 98209 04079
Mon to Sat 9am - 5pm. Closed 2nd and 4th Sat.

This trust provides meaningful work for over 30 mentally-challenged young adults. The inspirational centre, run by volunteers, is almost ten years old and makes wonderful eco-friendly products. The sturdy biodegradable leaf plates are really great and the gift bags, boxes and cards are delightful. *Cash only.*

⑪ WIT (Women's India Trust)

www.wit.org.in

23 Bombay Market, Tardeo
(nr AC Market, towards the back of the bldg).
Ph: 2351 1753
Mon to Sat 10am - 6pm.

Ms Kamila Tyabji established WIT in 1968 to train less privileged and unskilled women in Mumbai to stitch sari petticoats. The organisation now provides training and employment opportunities for thousands of women – helping women to help themselves. The shop has lovely hand-crafted goodies – toys, bags, tablecloths, laundry bags, bedspreads and even art.

⑫ Rehwa Society

www.rehwasociety.org

2 Ajit Villa, Ground Floor, Laburnum Rd, Gamdevi
(opp end of the street to Gandhi House).
Ph: 2380 3414
Mon to Frid 10.30am - 7pm, Sat 10.30am - 5pm.

This quarter-century old not-for-profit foundation, was created by the royal Holkar family of Indore. Rehwa's mission is to revive the centuries-old hand-weaving traditon of Maheshwar. 130 weavers produce over 100,000 metres of fine fabrics a year. Exquisite saris, shawls, stoles and yardage is available here from Rs.800 to Rs.6,000.

We recommend you support organisations that are socially and/ or environmentally sustainable, identified here with the Conscious Travel symbol (pg 149)

Mumbai is a shopper's
paradise, particularly
for women's clothing.

But whatever your
gender or age, you
are certain to find
your fancy.

Increasingly many
of the designers
are also extending
their skill into
homewares.

Use the codes below
to quickly find what
you are looking for...

C *(children)*

W *(women)*

M *(men)*

H *(home)*

Clothing & Textiles

LOCAL DESIGNER STUDIOS & BOUTIQUES

Abu Jani & Sandeep Khosla

"Loving Mother", 2 Om Chambers, Kemps Corner.
Ph: 2367 3401, 2367 3505
Daily 10.30am - 6.30pm. W

Abu and Sandeep are legendary figures in the Indian fashion scene; they have mentored countless young designers and are committed to reviving craft. They are known for intricate embroidered creations utilising Chikan embroidery from Lucknow and Zardozi, with fine gold- and silver- thread and exquisite sequin and beading work. Their clothes frequently appear on red carpets (most recently as worn by Dame Judi Dench at the Academy awards). In addition they do some interiors for clients including film star, Amitabh Bachchan (they even did a bedroom for Goldie Hawn in the Godrej house).

Ananya

Ground Floor, Burani Mahal, 59 Napean Sea Rd
(behind Kotak Mahindra Bank).
Ph: 5571 4888
Mon to Sat 11am - 8pm. W

Owned by sisters Nandita Mahtani and Anu Mirchandani this designer boutique is famous for hip, designer kurtas. These classic India tunics made from sheer fabrics with pretty embellishments have been worn by Madonna, Claudia Schiffer, Liz Hurley and Elle McPherson. Their London store in fashion-able Notting Hill is hugely popular with rich hippies. The clothing is classic fusion, feminine and sexy.

Other branch:

3, Pluto Bldg, Turner Rd, Bandra.
Ph: 2655 3327

⑨ amba by Hema Shroff Patel

Ph: 98211 50212
By appointment only. Malabar Hill. C W

Hema is a charming and talented textile designer who sells privately from her stunning Malabar Hill home, overlooking the Arabian Sea. Her passion developed while working with weavers at Rehwa Society and Women Weave, both non-profit weaving co-operatives. In 1999, she launched her own range of hand-woven clothing and divine accessories. Starting with children's pyjamas, called River Rompers, and designed for kids who *play, sleep, and dream*, Hema now has an extensive kids' clothing range, which is truly fabulous. She then went on to make River Rompers in adult sizes to keep the mums happy. They are comfortable, simple, and stylish. The adult range now extends to loungewear; sophisticated shawls and handbags crafted from wonderful textiles and antique brocade pieces. *Lovely!*

② D Block by James Ferreira

Hill Slope Bldg, Shop No A,
313 Zig Zag Rd, Pali Hill, Bandra (W).
Ph: 3268 8093 Mobile: 98215 21498
Daily 11.30am - 8pm.
James by appointment only. W

James has been a designer for over 35 years and is a much-loved personality in Indian fashion. He lives and works in the quaint historic village of Khotachi Wadi in his over-100-year-old family home. His small boutique is in fashionable Bandra.

James has an eclectic and ever-changing style; he is currently exploring natural fabrics and simpler styles, getting to the essence of good design. James has a sunny personality and his clothes have a warmth and gentle sense of fun. *Look out for the seamless collection, interesting and sexy!*

⑩ Geeta Khandelival

13 Altamount Rd,
Kemps Corner.
Ph: 2352 1275
Daily 11.30am - 8pm.
By appointment only. W H

Geeta runs an exclusive private boutique in her heritage home and carries unique designer pieces. She is an experienced Indian textile designer and highly creative.

Enjoy shopping for fun and fresh jewellery made from buttons; block-printed silk scarves, crocheted evening bags, patchwork quilts. Visiting her exquisite home is very special and the interior design endorses her beautifully-designed objects.

*Use the codes below
to quickly find what
you are looking for...*

C *(children)*
W *(women)*
M *(men)*
H *(home)*

LOCAL DESIGNER STUDIOS & BOUTIQUES (CONT'D)

❶ Mosaic & Kishmish
by Rekha Bhatia & Nikki Kalia

www.kishmish.in
5/9 Grant Bldg, Arthur Bundar Rd, Colaba
(above Barista Café).
Ph: 98200 17663
Mon to Sat noon - 7pm. By appointment. W

Rekha returned from her studies in the USA to pursue her passion for hand-woven naturally-dyed Indian textiles. She shared her mother's charming, large pottery studio; this creative space remains her base. Her brand Mosaic is now in its tenth year and is a collection of natural fibre shawls and stoles woven by villagers in central India. They range in price from Rs.2,500 to Rs.4,000 and come packed in beautiful fabric bags. Rekha believes in giving back to the weavers and is now on the design team for the NGO Women Weaves.

In 2006 Rekha partnered with her friend Nikki to create a clothing range in cool cottons for contemporary women. The range is designed to be simple, wearable and affordable with good cuts. The name Kishmish came from a childhood treat, a raisin, used as a reward for good behaviour. The clothes have a touch of whimsy and some lovely detailing, the button pockets and bags caught my attention.

①Narendra Kumar

The Courtyard, Shop No 5, S.P Centre.
Ph: 6638 5468
Daily 11am - 7pm. **W M**

Narendra was born and educated in Mumbai; he launched his own label in 1993 and is regarded as the intellectual of Indian fashion. He is seriously bright and is known for his social commentary and philosophy expressed through his fashion and controversial shows. He has taught fashion at NIFT, India's most prestigious institution; was the head designer at India's first premium fashion boutique; the founding editor of Elle, India's first fashion magazine; represented India at the Paris Design Biennale and does a significant amount of corporate work.

In amongst all of this he designs exciting and passionate fashion, and is popular with artists, actors and corporates. Narendra is a charming and generous person and continues to teach and work with under-privileged children. His legacy to Indian fashion is already hugely significant and you get the feeling the best is yet to come.

②Nikasha

www.nikasha.com

1 Carter Rd, Chimbai Village, Bandra (W).
Ph: 2640 0786 Mobile: 98870 16393
Mon to Sat 11am - 7pm.
Nikasha by appointment only. **W**

Visiting Nikasha in her sea-front studio nestled under a Peepal tree in a small fishing village is a fabulous Mumbai experience. Nikasha was born in Calcutta and studied to be a psychoanalyst before transitioning to design and settling into Mumbai. Her bohemian collection works with vintage Jaipur block prints. Nikasha is very proud of collaborating with Kitty, now 82 years old and one of the most-acclaimed print-makers in the country. The collection is feminine and very chic.

③The Yellow Leaf Company by Sonya Khan

Alvares House, Ground Floor, 188 Veer Savarkar Marg. (100 yards past the Hinduja hospital, adjacent to a small public park and Shirish Bldg, enter compound before traffic lights. Opp Bombay Scottish School) Mahim.
Ph: 2444 6126, 24454447
Mon to Sat 11am - 7.30pm. **W**

Sonya Khan left a prestigious and awarded career in advertising to pursue a dream to create fine classic clothing using natural fabrics. Struggling to find a name, she noticed a beautiful yellow leaf floated down and landed by her feet. Problem solved and The Yellow Leaf Company was named in 2001.

The store is tucked away in a 100-year-old building and houses a collection of fine, classic clothing in natural fabrics and a few stylish accessories. Sonya works with dyers, weavers and textile artisans across India and has a contemporary style with minimal embellishments. The collection changes frequently and you know you are buying something very special each time. Her signature staple is a very simple, flowing Nehru Jacket.

FASHION DESTINATIONS

SoBo

❶ Bombay Electric
www.bombayelectric.in

1 Reay House, B.E.S.T Marg, Colaba
(opp side entrance of Taj Mahal Hotel).
Ph: 2287 6276
Daily 11am - 9pm. W M

Deepak and Priya Kishore came to India
on holiday, were excited by the energy of
the city and saw an opportunity to create
an edgy vibrant design boutique fit for the
new India. The name reflects their thinking
of where India is today, a celebration of the
antique and the futuristic, a place where polar
opposites live in harmony, where rapid change
is coupled with ancient traditions.

Priya curates the eclectic collection based
on this thinking and showcases cutting-edge
work from over 20 Indian designers and ten
international designers. New collections arrive
every two weeks so there is always a freshness
and excitement about the store.

I was thrilled to see rare collectibles mixed
within the contemporary fashion. These tactile
treasures included a historic agate bracelet set
in solid silver for Rs.23,000. On the other end
of the spectrum are brightly coloured glass
bangles at Rs.200 for a dozen.

Their own range of clothing, Ghee Butter,
is soft, comfortable and stylish. The limited-
edition Bombay Electric T-shirts made from
100% Indian cotton are fabulous and there
are new colours every two months. The
Bombay Street Pack for men, two cotton
kurta tunics and two pairs of pants, custom
made, sells for Rs.2,500, is the essential
arrival clothing and a great idea. Indeed,
the tailoring service for men and women
has a great following.

LOCAL DESIGNER STUDIOS & BOUTIQUES (CONT'D)

❶ Tarun Tahiliani Boutique
www.taruntahiliani.com

Villar Ville, Ground Floor,
Ramchandani Marg, Apollo
Bunder, Colaba.
Ph: 2287 0895, 2285 4603
Daily 11am - 8pm. W M

Tarun is Indian glamour.
A fabulous Bombay story,
Tarun transitioned from a
family business in machine
tools and oil-field equipment
to creating luxury fashion.
He creates opulent, lavish
jewelled fashion and the
Mumbai flagship store is
located in a wonderful
heritage building overlooking
the Arabian Sea. There is
a special occasion menswear
collection, bridal collection
plus luxury accessories.

Other branch:

❷ Mi-Casa Junction of
St Theresa Rd, 28th Rd,
Bandra (W).
Ph: 2642 0643.

*Use the codes below
to quickly find what
you are looking for...*

❶ Ensemble

Great Western Bldg, 130/132 Shahid Bhagat
Singh Rd, Colaba (opp Lion Gate).
Ph: 2284 3227/5118, 2287 2882
Daily 11am - 7pm. **W M**

The forerunner of all designer stores in India
and still at the head. Ensemble carries a
comprehensive range from the best Indian
designers, doing fusion and classic Indian and
limited accessories and shoes. Very busy with
the weddings in town. The service is gracious
and intimate. Favourite designers include
Anamika Khanna from Kolkata, Monisha
Jaisingh and Tarun Tahiliani.

C *(children)*
W *(women)*
M *(men)*
H *(home)*

Other branch:

🔟 White Hall, Ground Floor, West Wing,
143 August Kranti Marg, Kemps Corner.
Ph: 2367 2416, 2367 2418.

A younger, hipper collection; open daily.

🔟 Mélange

www.melangeworld.com

Raj Mahal Bldg, 33 Altamount Rd, Kemps Corner.
Ph: 2353 4492, 2353 0288
Mon to Sat 10.30am - 7pm. **W**

Sangita Kathiwada selected the wine cellar
of a heritage building for Mélange. She has
used antique furniture pieces to create a very
special atmosphere in this exposed-brick,
stone-floored, cavern of a store. The 1,600
sq.ft. boutique is filled with contemporary
fashion and accessories for the Mumbai glam
girl scene. *Look out for the Metaphor brand by
Bangalore designer Chandrashekar (who did the book
marks for this book), exclusive to Mélange.*

🔟 Kimaya

www.kimayastudio.com

3 Delstar Building,
Kemps Corner (below
Kemps Cnr Flyover, next to
Crossword Books).
Ph: 2287 0895, 2285 4603
Daily 10.30am - 8.30pm. **W**

After opening in Juhu
in 2002 Kimaya has
expanded into SoBo. The
4,500 sq.ft. space celebrates
fashion extravagance.
The double-height space
has mirrored walls and
dazzling chandeliers to show
off India's largest collection
of designer fashion.

FASHION DESTINATIONS (CONT'D)

① The Courtyard

S.P Centre, 41/44 Minoo Desai Marg, Colaba
(nr Privé Club, around corner from Fariyas Hotel).
Daily 11am - 7.30pm. **W**

The Courtyard houses the pick of the Indian fashion scene in individual designer stores and has a beauty salon. *A lovely oasis to spend a few hours in (disappointing that there is no café). Must visit stores include:*

Tulsi by Neeru Kumar

Ph: 6638 5470 **W M H**

Delhi-based, *Neeru is one of the most highly regarded textile professionals in the country.* She successfully weaves traditional techniques with contemporary sensibility. A wonderful collection of daywear for women and men, plus a few wonderful vintage pieces.

Abraham & Thakore

www.abrahamandthakore.com
Ph: 6638 5486 **W M H**

Outstanding fashion with fabulously sensual and beautifully detailed clothes and accessories and homewares. *Mens shirts are stand-outs.*

Manish Arora Fish Fry

www.manisharora.ws
Ph: 6638 5486 **W**

Hip, young, hot, sexy, edgy and energetic fashion and bags and some wild sneakers, exclusively designed for Reebok. *This extrovert of a brand is making a splash globally.*

Rajesh Pratap Singh

Ph: 6638 5480, 6638 5481 **W M**

Highly-tailored design wear in luxurious fabrics for men and women.

Rabani & Rakha

www.rabaniandrakha.net
Ph: 5638 5476, 5638 5477 **W**

Superb saris and a store that brings to life the fantasy of Indian fashion.

Use the codes below to quickly find what you are looking for...

C *(children)*
W *(women)*
M *(men)*
H *(home)*

The Oak Tree

18 Colaba Causeway (nr Theobroma Café).
Ph: 2281 9031
Mon to Sat 11am - 8pm. W

A fun sparkly little fashion boutique. The glittery flip-flops are a must.

Other branch:

16th Rd, Bandra.
Ph: 2605 1959.

You

2 Cornelian, 104 A K Marg, Kemps Corner.
Ph: 2382 6972/73
Mon to Sat 10.30am - 7pm. W

A modern funky kitschy Indian designer shop for clothes, bags, shoes and jewellery. Renu Bothra began You in 2001 and her own eclectic range is at the shop along with eight local designers and more from across India. For fashion make sure to see Horn ok please, by Sabina Singh, Trupsel by Trupti Bellad, Mt Meru by Sushma Sakseria, Taxi by Aarti and Prachi and VSY by Viragi Shah.

FASHION DESTINATIONS

NoBo

Ayamik

Shop 1, Sea Palace,
Juhu Tara Rd.
Ph: 2660 7455
Daily 10.30am - 8.30pm. M

This quote by Jean Cocteau greets you on arrival: *'A man's style is his simple way of saying complicated things'*. This chic men's store was opened by the Kimaya team two years ago and only stocks Indian brands. Look for great shirts by local designer; Chirag Dattani and the male jewellery range by Bombay-based Sushma Cooper.

Barefoot

1st floor, Anand Villa, Palimala Rd, off Pali Hill, Bandra.
Ph: 3296 5067, 2648 0423
Daily 11.30am - 8.30pm. W H

This fresh chic shop is like a little piece of Goa in Mumbai. Enjoy browsing for fun fashion by young designers, trendy Kolhapuri sandals with a twist, and a good selection of accessories and Indian beauty products, including Ally Matthan fragrances and bath products, the Khadi Range and Forest Essentials.

Karma Kola

Bajaj Niwasm, Linking Rd, Khar (opp CKP Club).
Ph 3206 1063
Mon to Sat 11.30am - 9pm,
Sun 5.30pm - 9pm. W

This tiny store is the darling of the stylists and all the fashion magazines. Vivek Damani left advertising to join his fashion designer wife, Rekha, and launched the store in 2004. A bohemian shop celebrating kitsch with easily-affordable items for trendy young things. The Karma side of the store comprises the Indian textiles in western styles, including Om Shanty Baby, Rekha's line, plus other emerging Mumbai designers such as Trupsel and Yesha. The Kola side is western pop styles imported from Far East. There is also a selection of funky bags, shoes, belts and jewellery

*Use the codes below
to quickly find what
you are looking for...*

C *(children)*
W *(women)*
M *(men)*
H *(home)*

*We recommend you
support organisations
that are socially and/
or ennvironmentally
sustainable, identified
here with the Conscious
Travel symbol (pg149)*

FASHION DESTINATIONS (CONT'D)

20 Kimaya

2 Ahsa Colony, Juhu Tara Rd, Juhu
(opp Sea Princess Hotel).
Ph: 2660 5575, 2660 6154
Daily 10.30am - 8.30pm. W

Kimaya is a sophisticated store in North
Mumbai with over 100 of India's best fashion
brands. Neha and Pradeep Hirani launched
the store in 2002 and have created the
leading Haute Couture destination in the city.
One-stop shopping for Bollywood's leading ladies.

21 Zoya

A Gulistan Marg, Ground Floor,
184 D'Monte Park Rd off Turner Rd, Bandra (W)
(turn into lane opp the D'monte Park Club).
Ph: 2642 0888
Mon to Sat 11am - 8pm. C W M

Zoya was created in 2006 by three Mumbai
women who felt there was the need for a new
kind of store in North Mumbai. Zoya is a
chic, contemporary store housed in the ground-
floor of a beautiful bungalow. It is an intimate
calm space, 1,800 sq.ft. of India's celebrated
and stylish designers and has the best collection
of local talent in the city. Check out these
Mumbai designers:

Fashion: *Priyadarshini Rao, Lascelles Symons,
Deepika Gehani, Nalanda Bhandari, Gopi Vaid,
Nipa Badhiani, A Blue Lotus, Shilpa K and Risso.*

Jewellery: *Jamini Aluhwalia and Marium Khan.*

Handbag: *Malaga, Mandava, Divya A and
Vani Gupta.*

Footwear: *KAN, Veruschka and Crimson.*

Fabindia
www.fabindia.com

Jeroo Bldg, 137, M.G. Rd,
Kala Ghoda.
Ph: 2262 6539, 2262 6540
Daily 10am - 7.45pm.
W M C H

American John Bissell established Fabindia in 1960 to showcase Indian handloom textiles and provide employment to traditional artisans. The company now works with over 7,500 artisans from villages across India.

Fabindia carries textiles in a variety of natural fibres including ready-to-wear garments and accessories for men, women, teenagers and children; bed, bath, table and kitchen linen; floor coverings, upholstery fabric, and curtains. The home products range includes furniture, lights and lamps, stationery, pottery and cutlery. The organic food range, launched in 2004, supports local farmers. This flagship store is popular with travellers and locals and has Moshe's café on the upper level. *Fabindia is bursting with colour and energy. A delight.*

Other branches:

Noble House, Junction of Khar Danda Rd and 18th Rd, Khar (W).
Ph: 2605 7780, 2605 8622

Nos 2 & 4, Navroze, 66 Pali Hill, next to HDFC Bank, Bandra (W).
Ph: 2646 5286, 2646 5289

AUTHENTIC INDIAN

Anokhi
www.anokhi.com

Rasik Niwas, Metro Motor Lane, Dr. A. R. Rangnekar Marg, off Hughes Rd, Chowpatty.
Ph: 2368 5761, 2368 5308
Mon to Sat 10am - 7.30pm. W M C H

Anokhi had its beginnings in the late 60's when UK-based Faith Hardy came to Jaipur to meet tailors and block printers to create some clothing for friends who wished to open a shop in London. A small shop opened in Jaipur to sell off the excess export stock and there are now stores across India and in over ten other countries selling the fashionable easy-to-wear range. *Anokhi is a role model for ethical and environmental friendly business practices and the on-going revival of traditional textile skills.*

The *khadi* range is both hand-spun and hand-woven and perpetuates Gandhi's dream for a decentralised sustainable industry for India's rural population. Anokhi is another symbol of independent India and their range of clothing and accessories is excellent.

Other branch:

Govind Dham, 210 Waterfield Rd, Bandra (W).
Ph: 2640 8261, 2640 8263
Mon to Sat 11am - 8pm.

Use the codes below to quickly find what you are looking for...

C *(children)*

W *(women)*

M *(men)*

H *(home)*

AUTHENTIC INDIAN (CONT'D)

⑥ Khadi & Village Industries Emporium

286 Dr D N Rd, Fort.
Ph: 2207 3280 W M C H
Mon to Sat 10.30am - 6.15pm.

A government emporium that sells a wide range of products made by rural communities across India. The *khadi* range of ready-made clothes is a bargain and already very hip in the creative community. The full range of *khadi* beauty and bath products are available. The shop is from another era, old-fashioned displays and service, a complex shopping process and great value.

⑫ Neemrana Chikankari

www.thaidesigns.org

Purshotam Bdlg, 6, Ground Floor,
New Queen's Rd, Opera House, Girgaum.
Ph: 2361 4436, 2367 7780
Mon to Sat 10am - 8pm, Sun 11am - 7pm.
W M C H

A beautiful place to buy wonderful embroidered cottons from Lucknow. This stylish, pretty store has a lovely selection of cotton, georgette and silk kurtas (tunics) that are perfect for over-swimwear, over-jeans and travel well. Mens and childrens are also available, as are a limited selection of accessories and homewares. *One of the best shops in the city.*

Shrujan – Threads of Life
www.shrujan.org

Saagar Villa, 38 Bhulabahi Desai Rd
(opp Navroz Apt), Breach Candy.
Ph: 2352 1693
Mon to Sat 10am - 7pm. **W M H**

Shrujan formed in response to a famine relief project back in 1969 when a small group of women in Kutch, in the state of Gujarat, hand-embroidered saris to be sold in the city. From this modest start, Shrujan now works with 16 different styles of embroidery, done by 3,000 women across 100 villages. Since its inception, the not-for-profit trust has trained over 18,000 women giving them economic empowerment, generating confidence and respect. Shrujan has also built houses, organised cattle and health camps and been involved in relief efforts for natural disasters, including the massive earthquake of 2001. The Mumbai shop carries ethnic and western wear, home-accessories and gifts. Each is a unique piece of art, hand-embroidered by these women of Kutch. *A must-visit.*

INTERNATIONAL FASHION

Mumbai has plenty of international fashion brands ranging from Louis Vuitton to Levis, and Jimmy Choo to Nike. They are exactly as you would expect and you could be anywhere in the world. *However, there are two international fashion destinations that are unique to Mumbai...*

Muse
48 VB Gandhi Mar, Kala Ghoda
(opp Jewish Synagogue).
Ph: 6616 0000
Daily 11am - 8pm. **W M**

Opened in October 2007, this edgy international fashion store is located in a restored heritage building. The three-level space has impressive wooden staircases and high ceilings with original beams. The contemporary brands are exclusive to Muse in India. Owner, Tardini Jindal has expressed interest in special projects and collaborations with local designers, which would enrich this experience enormously.

Thanks
D Block, Shivsagar Estate,
Dr Annie Besant Rd, Worli.
Ph: 6616 0000
Daily 11am - 8pm. **W M**

Ashish Chorda has brought Dolce & Gabbana, Fendi, Chloe, Sergio Rossi and most recently Etro to India. His super-stylish emporium is the best example of luxury fashion-branding in the country, with exemplary service. The 10,000 sq.ft. space has a stretched artificial ceiling imported from France, and the walls are painted with automobile paint imported from Germany.

There is a whole floor dedicated to personal shopping and private catwalk shows. Ashish also represents Porsche India, which for his clientele, is considered just another accessory. Next, private jets?

*Use the codes below
to quickly find what
you are looking for...*

C *(children)*
W *(women)*
M *(men)*
H *(home)*

HANDBAGS

Meera Mahadevia
www.meeramahadevia.com

301/302 3rd Floor, Narayan Udyog Bhavan,
Lalbaug Industrial Estate, Lalbaug
(nr Parel).
Ph: 2471 1578, 2470 1554
Mon to Sat 10am - 6pm. W

*Meera has been making handbags for the Who's
Who of Indian style for the last twenty years.* She
identified a need for stylish, quality bags
that complemented clothing made from rich
Indian textiles. Her handcrafted bags are
contemporary in style and use fine Indian
craftsmanship. Often richly embellished, they
are intricate works of art and regarded as
heirloom pieces. Her work has found itself in
museums across the globe. Truly magnificent,
the range extends into belts, shoes and jewellery. Available from the studio and from the
following Mumbai designer stores:
Ensemble (pg55), Kimaya (pg68), and
Mélange (pg55).

SHOES

Prabhat Shoes
Ph: 98209 00413 W M

Mr Shyam Kale is a third-generation shoe-
maker. He is based in Pune and is regularly
in Mumbai taking orders for bespoke shoes
for Bollywood stars and Mumbai fashionistas.
He will meet you where you are staying
and designs to order, copying designs from
a magazine or catalogue or simply replacing
your loved shoes that are falling apart. He
is very proud of the cowboy boots, riding
boots, English brogues and fancy slippers.
*The workmanship and the value for money is
excellent.* Shoes start from Rs.2,500 and go
to Rs.20,000. Slipper and sandals start from
Rs.850. Unfortunately, his timing is a
little unreliable.

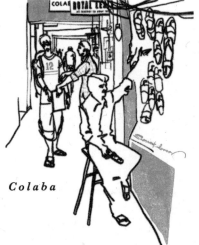

Colaba

SoBo

❶ Joy Shoes
Taj Mahal Palace & Towers Hotel,
Apollo Bunder, Colaba.
Ph: 2202 8696
Daily 10am - 7.30pm. W M

The most-famous and most-loved shoe shop
in the country. Started 65 years ago, Joy
produces handcrafted shoes for men and
women, from the finest Indian leather,
absolutely no synthetics are used. Many loyal
customers only buy their shoes from here. *Must
buys include the Swarovski slippers for Rs.3,950.*
Traditional hand-made Kolhapuri chappals are
available in many colours for Rs.990. Make sure
to see the footprint left by famous artist M.F.
Hussain, who often appears barefoot in public
and who redesigned the store in 2004.

❶ Corner Footwear
Beauty Corner Shoes
62, Balaji Bhavan, Colaba Causeway, Colaba
(opp Electric House, next to Nike).
Ph: 99693 94178 W M

Mr Husain Ali is a landmark himself, running
a very reputable street stall selling Kohlapuri
chappals for the best price (approx Rs.300)
in town.

❶ Rinaldi Designs
www.rinaldidesigns.com
67/69 Sea View Terrace,
118 B Woodhouse Rd, Colaba.
Ph: 2215 1394
Mon to Sat 11am - 7.15pm. W

Glitzy, sexy designer shoes
and now offering bespoke
shoes, so you get to choose
the fabric, heel and design
and they make them up for
you within a week.

❸ Gossip
66 The Oberoi Shopping
Centre, Nariman Point.
Ph: 2202 6946
Mon to Sat 10.30am - 8pm. W

Very popular, with stylish
Mumbai gals looking for
the latest in fashionable
slippers and heels. Make
sure to grab a few pairs
of the crystal slippers that
come in every colour of the
rainbow. Karim Jaffer also
owns Golden Touch next
door in the Hilton Towers
shopping centre with more
of the same.

NoBo

㉒ Moss
15A, Union Park,
(off Carter Rd), Khar (W).
Ph: 2646 0707
Daily 10am - 8pm. W

A small modern boutique
stocking stylish Indian brands
including Stoffa shoes. Moss
also has a wide range of
wonderful handbags. *The
hand-made cell phone bags are very
Mumbai and cost Rs.850.*

The Sari is an iconic symbol of India's grace and beauty; but for a traveller, they can seem daunting and confusing.

Contrary to what some foreigners believe, Indians encourage visitors to wear saris, just as western and fusion clothing are in the Indian woman's repertoire.

The Sari, six yards of beautiful fabric, can also be converted into wonderful clothes, curtains, cushions, and wall-hangings... do also ask to see shawls and dupattas, with equally enticing craftsmanship.

SARIS & SILKS

⑤ Kala Niketan

www.kalaniketangroup.com
85 Queens Rd, Churchgate.
Ph: 2200 5001
Mon to Sat 9.30am - 7pm. **C W M**

All roads lead to Kala Niketan when asking where to buy a sari in Mumbai. This institution has a rich heritage and is a wonderful shopping experience beginning with an ornate carved entry and garlanded deities. A footpath in Bombay was Jayantibhai's home in 1942, his first job was as a sales boy in a 200 sq.ft. sari shop called Kala Niketan. Over time his dreams and his talent enabled him to own the business, which now occupies 12,500 sq.ft. in the luxurious flagship store in Mumbai. There are now three other branches in India, including one in Juhu and a thriving export market.

Indian saris are as diverse as the country itself; this store has a comprehensive regional selection. Ask to be shown silks, brocades, embroidery and beadwork from across India. Also enjoy looking at fabric by the metre, jewellery and a full range of accessories.

① The Indian Textile Company

Taj Mahal Hotel, Apollo Bunder, Colaba.
Ph: 2202 8783
Mon to Sat 10am - 8pm. **W M H**

This company originated in Banares some 250 years ago and has a showroom at the Taj Hotel for the last 70 years. They have a wonderful collection of vintage textiles from Banares, Kashmir, Gujarat, Hyderabad and Rajasthan.

If you are a serious collector, establish prior contact to arrange an appointment to view the rare and valuable collection. Fabrics, saris, shawls, wall-hangings, bed covers and some ready-to-wear clothes are available in the showroom.

TAILORS –
WESTERN & INDIAN

❸ Leather Farm

F 96, H.C. Level, Oberoi Towers, Nariman Point.
Ph: 2285 6654
Mon to Sat 11am - 7pm. **W M**

Brothers Karim and Aly Jaffer tailor leather clothing to your designs. Bring your own inspiration or be inspired by magazines or what they have available in the small store front. Coats, pants, skirts are the main attraction, some handbags and luggage is available. Popular with flight crews and serious shoppers. *This business is 25 years old and is reliable and experienced. The prices are great, and turn-around time is generally only a few days.*

❶ Michele Boutique

21, Shah House, Mandlik Rd, Colaba
(opp State Bank & Indigo Restaurant).
Ph: 2287 0116, 2288 5312
Mon to Sat 10.30am - 8pm. **W M**

Nestled just behind the Taj Hotel this tailor has been in business for over three decades. He is very popular with flight crews who take their favourite suits, skirts and shirts to be copied. Turn around time is normally within a few days. A suit costs between Rs.8,000 and Rs.20,000 and a shirt approx Rs.1,000. Reliable, fast and good quality. *Especially good with linen.*

Use the codes below to quickly find what you are looking for...

C *(children)*
W *(women)*
M *(men)*
H *(home)*

⓮ Yaseen's

85 Sputnik, Bhulabhai Desai Rd, Breach Candy (opp Tata Garden, next to Standard Chartered Bank).
Ph: 2369 0272, 2364 1471
Mobile: 98210 70074
Mon to Sat 10am - 8pm. **W M**

A family-run business, founded in 1943, Yaseen's is a classic tailor with major industrialist and commercial figures as clientele. *Famous for bespoke suits that may be inspired by a magazine or copied from an old favourite.* Chose from English, Italian or Indian fabric and, ideally, allow up to three weeks for the suit to be completed. With charm, this time-frame can shorten to overnight or a few days. Excellent shirts.

Jewellery

HERITAGE

❸**Amrapali**
www.amrapalijewels.com
Shop 39 & 62, Oberoi
Shopping Centre, Nariman Pt.
Ph: 2284 3687, 2281 0978,
2282 0981
Mon to Sat 10.30am - 7pm.

Founded in Jaipur in 1978,
Amrapali celebrates the
tradition of Indian hand-
crafted jewellery. Amrapali
is globally-acclaimed and
is sought after by actors,
models and designers.

The collection contains
some exquisite heritage
pieces as well as a good
contemporary collection
inspired from all across the
country. *Shop 62 specialises
in gold, Shop 39 in silver.*

❻**Bhaghem Bombay**
38 Manglam House, Walchand
Hirachand Marg, Nr GPO, Fort.
Ph: 2261 7036, 2262 1016,
2262 6952
Mobile: 93233 20855
Mon to Sat 10.30am - 6.30pm.

Harish Chellani (Harry)
is a member of a family
business that was started
in 1967 and he is *the most
popular choice of the embassy
and expat crowd in Mumbai.*

Trusted for high-end jewellery design, he is well-known
and respected. His friendly
store also carries craft items
and carpets.

❶**The Gem Palace**
www.gempalacejaipur.com
The Courtyard, SP Centre,
41/44 Minoo Desai Marg, Colaba.
Ph: 6638 5484, 6638 5485
Mon to Sat 11am - 6pm.

The Gem Palace was established in 1852 by
the Kasliwal family of Jaipur. *Jewellers for over
eight generations, they have an extraordinary clientele
including royalty, Hollywood and Bollywood stars
and international designers.* The gem palace has
an impressive range of antique jewels from
the collections of maharajas to contemporary
designs studded with precious gemstones.

This family is involved in every field of
jewellery manufacturing, from the mining
of stones to designing and creating finished
fine jewellery. *World-famous, they are also the only
jewellery firm to be assigned a permanent display at
the Metropolitan Museum in New York.*

❻**Krishna Gems and Arts**
16 Rex Chambers, Walchand Hirachand Marg, Fort.
(opp India Dock, Red Gate, tucked away in a lane).
Ph: 2261 8673, 98200 51472
Mon to Sat 9.30am - 6pm.

Mr Krishna, affectionately known as the
'diamondwallah', has over 40 years experience.
He is very popular with expats, a favourite of
the British and Australian embassy staff and
offers a money-back
guarantee. He can come to you or will
arrange to collect you and guide you to
his office, and safely back home, with
your shopping.

❶**Tribhovandas Bhimji Zaveri**
241/43 Zaveri Bazaar, Kalbadev.
Ph: 2342 5001
Mon to Sat 10.30am - 7.30pm.

This long street is lined with dazzling stores,
a treasure-trove for the enthusiast. In business
since 1864, TBZ is the granddaddy of the
Zaveri jewellery bazaar. Spread over four
floors and popular with locals shopping for
gold and diamonds.

CONTEMPORARY

⑩ Zewar

Vasant Vihar, 8 M. L Dahanukar Marg
(Carmichael Rd, off Pedder Rd, close to
the Belgian Embassy), Kemps Corner.
Ph: 2351 5794. By appointment.

Jamini Ahluwalia pioneered the concept of
costume jewellery in India in the 1980s. Her
style is eclectic, mixing different raw materials
like metal, silk, wood, and stones. Many of
the city's well-heeled favour her bold creations
over their own diamonds and some wear
her jewellery exclusively. Recently, Jamini
has branched into homeware with curtain
tiebacks, tassles and napkin rings. Popular
with Bollywood designers, fashion stylists
and increasingly a global market.

*Visiting the studio located in Jamini's family home is
a lovely experience.* As well as the jewellery and
homewares there is also a wonderful range
of shawls. Cash only. The premium jewellery
range is exclusively available at **Bungalow 8
(pg45)** and **Zoya (pg58)**.

⑭ Stoned by Anita

803, Mazda, Warden Rd, Breach Candy.
Ph: 98216 34833
By appointment only.

Anita Vaswani has had a lifelong passion for
gemstones. Her father is a gemologist and
gem-trader and her mother is a jewellery
designer. Anita launched Stoned in Mumbai
in 2004 and the brand is gaining recognition
both in her birthplace, New York, and in her
motherland, India.

Like Anita, the jewellery is sexy, modern and
global, and the collection has an easy-to-wear
aesthetic and affordable price tags.

The *'Highly Stoned'* range
has beautiful gemstones set
in sterling silver. *'Cosmica'*
is a spiritual collection
made up of sterling silver
charms and *rudraksha* beads
combined with beautiful
semi-precious stones such
as coral and blue topaz.
'Bombay Princess' is a
collection styled in the
technique of art deco
and Maharaja chic; or
in Anita's words *'rich
Indian decadence'!*

Stoned is available
privately and retails at:
**Bombay Electric (pg54),
D Block (pg51),
Neemrana (pg60)** and
Oak Tree (pg57).

FUN

⑭ Vividha

23, Chandra Lok "A", 97
Napean Sea Rd (back of bldg),
Breach Candy.
Ph: 2369 6185
Mon to Sat 10am-8pm.

Bangles, Bindis and Bling.
Since 1972 this family-
owned shop has been the
place to come for Indian
accessories, all locally
manufactured. Prices range
from Rs.10 to Rs.500.

Home

ANTIQUES

1 D. Popli & Sons

Readymoney Bldg,
Battery St, Colaba,
(behind Regal Cinema).
Ph: 2202 1694, 2204 2055
Mon to Sat 10am - 8pm,
Sunday 1pm - 5pm.

Established in 1928 and still
proudly family-owned and
famous for antique silver.

1 Essajee's

Ground Floor, Lansdowne
House, Battery St, Colaba
(behind Regal Cinema,
next door to Gordon House
Boutique Hotel).
Ph: 2202 1071, 2285 1807
Mon to Sat 11am - 6pm.

A treasure-trove. An Aladdin's
cave of exotic things,
ranging from large furniture
to paintings and trinkets.
This store is just the tip
of the iceberg. A trip to
the warehouse can also
be arranged.

1 Famroz Sorabji Khan & Co.

Chhatrapati Shivaji Marg, Colaba
(along from Regal Cinema).
Ph 2202 1638
Mon to Sat 11am - 6pm.

Family-owned little store packed with an
assortment of small antiques and bric-a-brac.

4 Natesans Antiquarts

www.natesans.com

Jehangir Art Gallery, Basement, MG Rd.
Ph: 2285 2700
Mon to Sat 10am - 7.30pm.

A wonderful golden place in the basement
of Bombay's most-loved gallery. Natesans is
a family firm that began business in Kerala
over seven decades ago. A quiet passion for
beautiful things and wonderful craftsmanship
is evident.

*This is the place to pick up a treasured artifact,
commission a piece of art and begin falling in love
with India.* Natesans began by manufacturing
fancy ivory buttons and is now credited with
pioneering the dealing in antiques, which
became a hot hobby in pre-independence
India and remains so today.

Shop for antique oil lamps, spice boxes and
statuettes of Hindu deities, plus stunning
larger pieces, including wonderful woodcarv-
ings, stone and bronze sculptures. Note
however, that most antiquities cannot leave
the country without the permission of the
Archaeological Survey of India. Natesans is
a well-respected, trustworthy dealer and can
guide you through shipping and customs.

Other branch:

1 Taj Mahal Hotel,

Colaba.

Phillips
www.phillipsantiques.com
Opposite Regal Cinema, Museum, Colaba.
Ph: 2202 0564, 2282 0782
Mon to Sat 10am - 7pm.

Phillips, established in 1860, is the oldest
antique shop in the city and is fiercely proud
of this long heritage. It is a beautiful store
with a powerful aesthetic. This fourth-genera-
tion family concern is a collector's paradise,
the Issa family admitting that they are incor-
rigible collectors. You can find true magic
in the store, ranging from French glasses to
silver Chinese filigree dolls house furniture.
An exhilarating shopping experience

*I am particularly excited by the growing emphasis on
Indian tribal art and collectible craft and am looking
forward to the new store that Phillips will open in
2008 focused on this.*

The 18 **Planter's Chair** is a division of
Phillips antiques and carries a large range of
decorative old furniture, located in a 5,000 sq.
ft. warehouse in Wadala (E) about 40 mins
from Colaba. Ph: 2412 1929.

Phillips Images
www.phillipsimages.in

Located in a laneway at the back of the
Phillips main store, opposite the Sahakari
Bhandar shop on the causeway and through
the gate of the Oriental Mansion.

Phillips has converted their old *"godown"*
warehouse into a specialist gallery and shop
for reprints from their collection of litho-
graphs, engravings, old maps and photographs
from the 16th to 19th centuries. The earliest
map in the collection dates back to 1560.
The offering is thoughtful, with ready-made
prints, framed limited editions and a service
to reproduce the images to the size required.
Excellent.

Heeramaneck & Son
Readymoney Bldg,
Battery St, Colaba
(behind Regal Cinema).
Ph: 2285 6340, 2202 1778
Mon to Sat, 10am - 8pm, Sun
1pm - 5pm.

Established over 30 years
ago, Heeramaneck is a
high-end traditional store
with exquisite period silver
and objets d'art.

Pukhraj Jawanal Surana
47, Dagina Bazaar,
Mumbadevi Rd.
Ph: 2242 4416/2242 4738
Mon to Sat 10am - 1.30pm,
2pm - 7.30pm.

PJS is a small gem of shop
selling old silver – tea sets,
frames, boxes, dishes, napkin
rings. The great-grandson
of the founder runs
this well-respected shop.
*Remember to shop comparatively,
check out the neighbouring shops
price per gram of silver, noting
that silver is primarily sold on
weight, not craftsmanship, and
do bargain hard in this part of
town.*

Chor Bazaar – The Thieves Market, Mutton St.

No guide to antique shopping in Mumbai could miss the famed Chor Bazaar.

It is a wonderful adventure to explore the alleys and lanes searching for treasures amongst the 'real fake antiques'. Visit between 11am and 7pm. On Fridays many of the shops close, whilst a flea market takes over.

Chor Bazaar

My favourite Chor Bazaar stores include:

Chandeliers & Furniture house is run by the Mansuri Brothers, 18 Mutton Street – wonderful glass, including French chiffoniers, a whimsical delight. Ph: 2341 2378.

Batiwalla & Co at 38 Mutton Street – a mature man who had been dealing in bottles and objects for a lifetime, running a tiny hole-in-the-wall store. I picked up two Portuguese coffee bowls.

Mr Zafar who runs **Jubilee Decorators** at 127-129 Mutton Street has marble statues which hip hoteliers snaffle up for their Goan properties, great furniture, paintings and also charming hand-painted miniatures that make perfect gifts. Ph: 2347 6699.

Bollywood Bazar is a specialist store trading in Bollywood Posters, Lobby Cards, Photo Stills and Synopsis Booklets from the 1930s to 1950s. They also have some excellent authentic vintage bits and pieces. Ph: 2347 2427.

CONTEMPORARY ART

The essential Mumbai Galleries:

⑥ Chemould Prescott Road

www.gallerychemould.com

Queens Mansion, 3rd Floor,
G. Talwatkar Marg, Fort.
Ph: 2200 0211, 2200 0212, 2200 0213
Mon to Sat 11am - 7pm.

Established in 1963 by Kekoo and Khorshed Gandhy, Chemould is one of India's oldest commercial galleries and has nurtured modern and contemporary Indian art by supporting young talent. Shireen Gandhy took over as the director of the gallery from her parents in 1988. She added dynamism by spearheading a focus on young emerging artists with an experimental and interdisciplinary approach to practice and media. In February 2007, the Gallery Chemould moved into a new space – Chemould Prescott Road. This 5,000 sq. ft. gallery has state-of-the-art facilities and is housed in a 100-year-old British colonial building with high ceilings and spectacular views of Mumbai's heritage architecture. Renewed and reinvigorated, Chemould is 43 years young.

① Sakshi Gallery

www.sakshigallery.com

Tanna House, Ground Floor, 11A Nathalal Parekh Marg, Colaba (in the Regal Cinema vicinity).
Ph: 6610 3424
Mon to Sat 11am - 7pm.

Situated in a leafy tree-lined avenue on the ground-floor of an old quintessentially Colaba building with its own garden and portico. This is the third home for this 20-plus-year-old gallery. Sakshi is the largest private gallery in the country and has an exciting programme of established and emerging artists. The gallery has an art advisory section, an art lending library for corporate houses and undertakes large public commissions, besides supporting students and young artists with scholarships.

Mumbai has a vibrant contemporary art culture. There has been a boom in Indian art since 2000, with strong global interest and record-breaking prices.

Mumbai is regarded as the Manhattan of Indian art – with Kala Ghoda being the Chelsea, the epicentre of the contemporary art scene. This art district has over twenty galleries.

Begin exploring this area at the ① *National Gallery of Modern Art (open Tues to Sat, 11am - 6pm) then head to the* ④ *Jehangir that has four public galleries and the loved Café Samovar, (pg19); then explore the streets of Kala Ghoda and beyond... Mumbai Magic are developing guided art walks in the city (pg101).*

CONTEMPORARY ART (CONT'D)

17 Saffron Art
www.saffronart.com

Industry Manor, 3rd Floor,
Prabhadevi, Worli
Ph: 2436 4113
Mon to Sat 10am - 7pm.

A comprehensive resource for modern and contemporary Indian art, www.saffronart.com is the first website on Indian contemporary art to offer access to aggregated, comprehensive content on-line along with an extensive catalogue of Indian art available for purchase via auction and direct sale.

1 Galerie Mirchandani + Steinruecke
www.galeriems.com

2 Sunny House, 16/18 Mereweather Rd, Colaba (behind Taj Hotel and off road entrance, behind lifestyle shop, Apartment 9).
Ph: 2202 3030, 2202 3434, 2202 3636
Mon to Frid 10am - 6.30pm, Sat 11am - 4pm.

A sophisticated new gallery displaying progressive art, both Indian and international. In addition a good collection of India's pre-eminent artists.

1 Project 88
www.project88.in

BMP Bldg, Ground Floor, N.A.Sawant Marg, Colaba (nr Colaba Fire Station).
Ph 2281 0066, 2281 0099
Tues to Sat 10.30am - 6.30pm,
Mon 2.30pm - 6.30pm.

An interesting, edgy gallery in Mumbai, which is an offshoot of the prestigious Galerie 88 in Kolkata. Sree Banerjee Goswami, daughter of Galerie 88 founder, Supriya Banerjee, is looking after the Mumbai chapter and has brought fresh energy to the art scene.Located in a century-old metal printing press that has been restored and redesigned by heritage architect Rahul Mehrota, the industrial aesthetics provide an exciting environment to showcase contemporary art and exciting multi-media performances.

4 Bodhi Art
www.bodhiart.in

28, K. Dubash Marg, I.T.T.S. House, Kala Ghoda (opp. Jehangir Gallery).
Ph 6610 0125
Mon to Sat 11am - 7pm,

Bodhi Art is synonymous with the global boom in Indian contemporary art. Bodhi Art showcases over 40 of India's best artists and has a full exhibition programme at the Mumbai and Delhi gallery spaces. In addition, Bodhi has established galleries in New York and Singapore and has taken Indian contemporary art to new audiences. Bodhi is active in its support for their artists and undertakes residencies, outreach programmes and public art projects.

① Chatterjee & Lal
www.chatterjeeandlal.com

C&L Gallery, 01/18 Kamal Mansion Floor 1,
Arthur Bunder Rd, Colaba (nr Radio Club),
Ph: 6521 5105
Mon to Sat 11am - 7pm.

Mortimer Chatterjee, curator, dealer, art advisor and his partner, Tara Lal, have just launched *Mumbai's newest gallery space* in a heritage building in Colaba, integrating original architectural details with state-of-the-art lighting and audio visual equipment. The gallery features international and local artists and is committed to new media works. *A showcase for video, installation and performance-based art.*

⑥ Gallery Beyond
www.gallerybeyond.in

130/132 First Floor, Great Western Bldg,
Shahid Bhagat Singh Marg, Fort.
Ph: 2283 7345
Mon to Sat 11am - 7pm.

This gallery showcases young Indian artists and is located in the historic Great Western Building near the Naval dockyards of Mumbai. Constructed in 1847, the building housed the East India Company and at one stage was the Carlton Hotel. Gallery Beyond is on the first-floor, which used to be ballroom, and has a fabulous Spanish tiled floor. On the floor above is another gallery, Hacienda. *On the way here, make sure to see the Brinda Miller murals on the dockyard walls, depicting the history of Bombay.*

⑥ The Fourth Floor
Kitab Mahal, 192 D N Rd, Fort (New Book Co Bldg, opp Central Camera Company, nr VT).
Ph: 2207 9119, 2207 1771, 2207 4772
Mon to Sat 11am - 7pm.

This gallery and cultural centre, opened in 2005, is a sprawling interesting space in a vintage building and has an interesting calendar of events – films, plays and exhibitions.

① Superior Frames
146 SBS Rd, Colaba
(opp Colaba Bus Station,
 next to Post Office).
Ph: 2216 5888
Daily 9am - 9pm.

When visiting project 88 and C&L, make sure to pop into this little framing studio in Colaba. *Discover a classic Bombay story.* Chenaram Kumar arrived in Mumbai 20 years ago from a small village in Rajasthan; he was only 16 years old and was trying to find his way in the metropolis. He got a few odd jobs and then was given a chance by Shanty Chopra, the owner of Art Musings gallery. She lent him a small sum of money to start his own framing business.

Chenaram thrived along with the Indian art world and continues to do work for leading galleries and artists. He delights in showing his personal collection of signed originals from India's leading artists.

Everyone who comes to India wants to buy a carpet and then gets lost in a whirl of confusion.

Do some homework first, what size, what material and what price range. A popular size is the 6 ft x 4 ft as it can work in most rooms on the floor or as a wall hanging.

A good tip from a GM of a luxury hotel was to learn about quality and the price ranges at the government fixed-priced emporiums before venturing to the private dealers, who will have a better range.

Both of the entries here are strong recommendations from Mumbai locals who have been loyal customers for many years.

CARPETS

16 Qayoom Kashmiri

27/33, Mazagaon Terrace, Nesbit Rd, nr Byculla.
Ph: 2373 0221 Mobile: 986762 1975,
98190 93680

A friend in Malabar Hill was persuaded to part with the name of her *'carpetwallah'* who has been looking after her and her family for decades. Mr Kashmiri is from Srinigar and moved to Mumbai over 30 years ago. He is still working with his family based in the mountains, who have been in the carpet business for over 100 years. He is an absolute authority on carpets, selling Persian, Afghanistan and Indian, silk, wool and fabulous kilims.

He will come to you or arrange to meet you in his tiny, basic show room at home. Also ask to see his marvellous authentic Pashminas. They range from about Rs.700 to Rs.60,000 depending on the embroidery.

17 Mehra Carpet Manufacturers

Crystal, 70 Dr. Annie Besant Rd, Worli.
Ph: 2493 2254, 2493 2998, 2493 6389
Mon to Sat 10.30am - 7pm.

Mr Sharma, the manager, and Ramesh, who showed me the carpets, started at MCM on the same day 37 years ago and together have watched the business grow. They have carpets ranging from Rs.8,000 to over Rs.1,000,000. Choose from silk-on-silk, silk-on-cotton, wool, kilims or dhurries.

FURNITURE

16 Pinakin
www.pinakin.in

2nd Floor,Raghuvanshi Mills Compound,
Senapati Bapat Marg, Lower Parel.
Ph: 6600 2400, 6600 2500
Mon to Sat 10.30am - 7pm.

Pinakin Patel, architect and interior designer,
lives and works in the idyllic haven of
Alibaug, a one-hour ferry ride from the
city. He does major design projects for his
sophisticated clientele in Alibaug and in
the city.

This contemporary Indian furniture store is
widely regarded as the best in the city. The
Brahmaputra dining table is a classic, made
from oak wood and granite with a water
channel for candles and flowers. Priced at
Rs.88,000 it is tempting to pack and ship it,
which of course can be easily be arranged.

17 Pallate
Badamiya Manor, 34 Clerk Rd, off Racecourse
Rd, Mahalaxmi (take second on right after the
Willingdon Club, with race course on your left).
Ph: 2498 3575, 2498 3556
Mon to Sat 10.30am - 7.30pm.

A design super studio, across 33,000 sq.ft.
and four floors, displaying contemporary
Mumbai living. Presenting award-winning
furniture and homewares from across the
world, with one floor devoted exclusively
to Indian design, including accessories from
the acclaimed Mukul Goyal.

18 The East India Company - Interiors
www.theeastindiacompany.com

The New Great Eastern Mills,
25/29 Dr Ambedkar Rd,
Byculla.
Ph: 98204 55721,
98691 64813
Mon to Sat 10.30am - 7.30pm,
Sun 11.30am - 6.30pm.

A wonderful chance to see a
mill complex, complete with
its own pond with turtles
and ducks. Drive through
the mill buildings to the
rear to visit the sophisticated
interior shop spread over
9,000 sq.ft. selling Indian
furniture, art and artifacts.
Ask to see the workroom
located back in the mill,
where 60 artisans are at
work creating furniture.

Anurag Kanoria is the
enthusiastic owner of
the home business, his
grandfather owns the mill,
and Anurag's father is
developing the mill into a
residential complex.

① Chunilal Mulchand & Co

Indian Mercantile Mansion,
Madame Cama Rd (opp Museum), Colaba.
Ph: 2202 0494, 5604 2129
Mon to Sat 10am - 7pm.

Mumbai was the home of Indian cotton. Set up in 1925, this down-to-earth store is known for quality and value. Come here for pure white Indian cotton bed linen (if not in stock the tailoring will take two or three days). *Make sure you know your bed size in detail, simply saying King or Queen will not work here.*

① Dit

1A Glamour House, Shahid Bhagat Singh Rd,
Colaba (opp Standard Auto Services).
Ph: 2283 2523

Josephine Mendes (pet name was Dit) opened the store in 1942 and her charming son Frank now runs it. Everything is hand-made by nuns and orphans; bed spreads, tablecloths, handkerchiefs and plenty in-between. *Perfect place to stock up for your wedding trousseau.*

SOFT FURNISHINGS & LINENS

① Atmosphere

www.himatsingka.com
Vaswani House,
7 Best Marg, Colaba.
Ph: 2283 1877
Mon to Sat 10.30am - 7.30pm.

Atmosphere is India's finest luxury home-furnishing brand. The quality and design are stunning as are some of the prices. Upholstery, curtain and blind fabrics, mainly silk, are sold by the metre and staff will recommend tailors. Another branch in Santa Cruz.

④ India Weaves

www.india-weaves.com
72 Bhulabhai Desai Rd, Breach Candy,
(nr Cymroza Art Gallery, opp Amarson Estate).
Ph: 2368 6366, 6572 3156
Mon to Sat 10am - 8pm.

Majestic silks for home furnishings, by the metre or order made-to-measure. Make sure to bring detailed measurements of your requirements and they will make up curtains, bed coverings and cushions. *You can save up to 70% on European or North American prices.*

Furtados

①Soma
www.somashop.com

A2, Amar Chand Manion, 16 Madam Cama Rd, Colaba (above Golden Gate Restaurant).
Ph: 2282 6050
Mon to Sat 10am - 8pm.

Soma is a Jaipur-based organisation specialising in reviving and promoting the craft of block-printing on 100% Indian cotton. *Since 1984, Soma has provided employment to over 300 families involved in the production of these lovely textiles.* As well as home furnishings, there is a lovely selection of craftwork, fashion and accessories. Great children's range.

①Yamini
www.yamini-stores.com

President House, Wodehouse Rd, Colaba.
Ph: 2218 4143
Daily 10.30am - 7.30pm.

This store is stylish and colourful, selling upholstery and curtain fabric by the metre and ready-to-use products for table, bed and bath. All purchases come in great fabric carry-bags. Yamini is popular with interior designers and was selected to create the interiors of the presidential planes.

Et cetera
MUSIC
⑪Furtado & Co
www.furtadosmusic.com

540/4 Kalbadevi Rd (opp Metro Cinema), Kalbadevi.
Ph: 2201 3163, 2201 3105, 2201 2756
Mon to Sat 10am - 7.30pm.

Furtados is proud of its 140-year-old history, selling Indian instruments, sitars and tablas for thousands of rupees plus a selection of small Indian instruments – get a gungroo, the ankle bracelet with bells for Rs.125 or a simple wooden flute like Krishna's for Rs.30 or a dumroo (monkey drum) for Rs.95. There is also a large collection of religious statues which makes an interesting backdrop for teenagers jamming on electric guitars. *Just around the corner pop into the Irani café, Kyani (pg20) ideal for a chai break.*

④Rhythm House
www.rhythmhouseindia.com

40 K Dubash Marg, Kala Ghoda, Fort.
Ph 2284 2835
Mon to Sat 10am - 8.30pm, Sun 11am - 8.30pm.

THE music shop in the city. Stocking a great collection of Indian music, classical, spiritual, sound tracks and Hindi pop. Look out for the Bombay Lounge music. The staff is extremely knowledgeable and helpful.

FOOD & COOKWARE

⑪Crawford Market
Mon to Sat 11am - 8pm

The best food shopping remains at this historic market located on Lokmanya Tilka Marg and Dr D. N. Road, Fort. For photography, catch the early-morning light on produce being unpacked. Make sure to wander through to the rear of the market to see the abundance of fresh produce, particularly wonderful in mango season just before the monsoon. Rudyard Kipling's father, who ran an art school in Bombay, did the lovely friezes on the exterior of the purpose built market, constructed in 1865. Nearby is the Utensil Market.

⑪Mangalam Steel
Daily 10am - 8pm
Ph: 2242 7421

A great place to buy tiffin tins and Indian cookware, located at 126, Kansara Chawl, Kalbadevi Road.

In SoBo, *Indigo Deli (pg21)* Colaba, is the best place for gourmet cookware, food, wine and takeaway options. *The Bakery* at the Taj Mahal Palace Hotel *(pg140)* and *Theobroma (pg24)* on the causeway are also good options for snacks.

In NoBo, *The Gourmet Store* at the Grand Hyatt *(pg146)* is fabulous.

⑯Conscious Food
www.consciousfood.com

318 Vasan Udyog, Lower Parel
(opp the entry to Phoenix Mills).
Ph: 3343 5965, 3245 3444
Mon to Sat 10am - 6pm.

Soul food and safe food. Started in 1990 in Mumbai by eco-nutritionist Kavita Mukhi, Conscious Food is a natural and organic food producer committed to healthy foods, traditional small farmers and uncompromising quality. The range has over 100 products and includes cereals, power-snacks, beverages, herb and spices, natural oils, salts and sweeteners. The chai is particularly good, as are the peppermint drops.

Visit the workshop or pick up from Indigo Deli *(pg21)*. Stockists and a full catalogue are available on the website.

WINE

⑪Shah & Co
www.shahwines.com

Sitaram Bldg, Ground Floor
(opp Police Commissioners Office,
nr Crawford Market), Kalbadevi.
Ph: 2347 7121
Mon to Sat 10am - 8.30pm.

Reputed to be the best wine shop in India. Shah has a great range, good prices and good storage conditions. Started by Iranis in 1904, Mr Munjral took over the store in 1958; it is now run by his 36-year-old son, Randip, a knowledgeable and approachable wine enthusiast. *A fine place to learn about and buy Indian wine.*

FLOWERS

⑩ Bageecha

Moyilal Mansion, 17 Napean Sea Rd
(next to Contemporary Arts and Crafts),
Kemps Corner.
Ph: 2367 7008
Daily 8am - 7pm.

This 28-year-old street-side florist has a fabulous reputation and does the flowers for many Mumbai socialites and some of the most stylish shops and restaurants in the city, including Indigo and Vong Wong. Credit cards accepted.

MISCELLANEOUS

OPTICAL GLASSES

⑥ Lawrence & Mayo

www.lawrenceandmayo.co.in

274 Dr. Dadabhai Naoroji (D N) Rd, Fort.
Ph: 2207 6049, 2207 6051
Daily 11am - 2pm, 4pm - 9pm.

Spectacles are a bargain in India, often half the price of those in Europe or the USA. Make sure to bring your prescription and head to a trusted optician. Lawrence and Mayo, founded in 1877, is the oldest in India.

BITS & BOBS

㉑ Something Special

63 Hill Rd, Bandra (W).
(opp St. Joseph Convent High School).
Ph: 2642 2526, 2643 0894
Mon to Sat 9am - 2pm, 3pm - 9pm, Sun 9am - 11am.

This is a special find, jammed-packed with everything, buttons and bows, sequin ribbon to feather boas. Toys and art materials. A fabulous haberdashery shop that makes anyone feel creative.

BUSINESS CARDS

㉑ Durga Arts Designers and Printers

G1 & 2, Dunhill Dome, St John Rd, nr Pali Naka, Bandra (W).
Ph: 2651 5194, 2651 6015
Mobile: 98210 27397

Business cards are a bargain in India. Mr Deepak Malhotra of Durga does an excellent job. The charges depend upon the design you select. For 200 cards, expect to pay Rs.800 for something simple and up to Rs.1,300 for something with more colour, printed both sides.

PHARMACY

③ Royal Medico

Shop 7, Lobby, Hilton Tower, Nariman Point.
Ph: 6582 1639
Mon to Sat 9.30am - 8.30pm,
Sun 9.30am - 6.30pm.

An excellent pharmacy if you are feeling poorly or simply want to stock up on Ayurvedic products from the Himalaya Drug Company, Kama or Forrest Essentials *(pg91)*.

④ Marg Publications
www.marg-art.org

Army & Navy Bldg, 3rd Floor, 148 M.G Rd, Kala
Ghoda (above Westside Showroom, opp Jehangir
Art Gallery), Kemps Corner.
Ph: 2284 2520, 2282 1151
Mon to Frid 9.30am - 5.30pm.

The philosopher and social activist Mulk
Raj Anand founded Marg in 1946 to
raise awareness and preserve India's
cultural heritage. Marg continues to publish a
quarterly magazine and a range of excellent
books on India's monuments, crafts, culture
and civilisation.

The website has a full listing of titles and the
office in Mumbai carries some stock. Purchases
at the office receive a 20% discount. Credit
cards accepted.

⑩ Motilal Banarsidass
8 Mahalakshmi Chambers, 22 Bhula Shai Desai Rd.
Ph: 2351 3526, 2351 6583, 3092 2105
Mon to Sat 10am - 7pm.

Leading Indian publisher on Sanskrit and
Indian studies since 1903, with an impressive
range of scholarly publications.

④ Chetana Book Centre
34 K. Dubash Marg, Kala Ghoda
(opp Jehangir Art Gallery).
Ph: 2285 3412
Mon to Sat 11am - 7.30pm.

Chetana has over 3,000 titles covering
philosophy, religion, arts, culture and Indian
thought. Plus, a comprehensive selection on
health, well-being and alternative medicine.
The vegetarian café next door is an ideal place
to begin page one!

⑪ New and Second-Hand Bookshop
526 Kalbadevi Rd (nr Metro Cinema), Kalbadevi.
Ph: 2201 3314
Mon to Sat 10am - 7.30pm.

Mr Vishram presides over this 100-year-old
store that his grandfather founded. I enjoyed
browsing and buying second-hand travel books,
some gems for sure. Cash only.

Reading

BOOKS, MAGAZINES & NEWSPAPERS

Independent Book Stores:

⑥ Strand Book Stall
www.strandbookstall.com

"Dhannur", Sir P.M. Rd, Fort.
Ph: 2266 1719
Mon to Sat 10am - 8pm.

A well-established shop that
has character, albeit not a
Daunts (London, UK) or a
Pilgrims (Kathmandu).

It is on two levels and has
a great selection of Indian
books and authors,
a permanent discount
of 20% on all books and
friendly knowledgeable staff.

Hotel Book Stores:

①Nalanda Book & Record Shop

Shopping Centre, Taj Mahal Hotel,
Apollo Bunder, Colaba.
Ph: 2202 2514, 2287 1306
Daily 8am - midnight.

A compact store that has everything that a
traveller may need. A comprehensive Indian
collection of coffee table books, travel guides
and novels. Excellent magazines and newspapers. Good postcards, DVDs and music CD's.

③Ritika

Oberoi Nariman Point.
Ph: 2284 3761
Daily 9.30am - 10pm.

A small and glossy store of hand-selected books
that celebrate India and a five-star collection
of international magazines and newspapers.

Other branch:

②Taj President Hotel, Cuffe Parade.
Ph: 2215 0124

National Chains

⑩Crossword

www.crosswordbookstores.com

Mohammed Bhai Mansion, N. S. Marg, Kemps Cnr.
Ph: 2384 2001
Mon to Frid 11am - 8.30pm, W'end 11am - 9pm.

The Barnes and Noble of India. The broadest
range of books and magazines in the city
displayed in an excellent environment.
Moshe's café on the first floor is a popular
meeting place.

⑤Oxford Bookstore

www.oxfordbookstore.com

Apeejay House, 3 Dishna Vachha Rd, Churchgate.
Ph: 6636 4477
Daily 10am - 10pm.

A good collection of mainstream books with
a strong children's collection. The Chai Bar
serves a wide choice of tea and is a nice
place to enjoy your purchases. A popular
venue for book launches and author signings,
with a selection of autographed best-sellers.

HAND-MADE PAPER

⑥Chimanlals

www.chimanlals.com

A 2 Taj Bldg, 210 Dr D N Rd
(enter from Wallace St, Fort.
opp New Excelsior Cinema).
Ph: 2207 7717, 2207 4764
Mon to Frid 9.30am - 6pm,
Sat 9.30am - 5.30pm.

*This lovely shop opened in
1974 and has become a
Mumbai institution.* The
popular designs are rooted
in Indian culture and
the range includes social
stationery and gift-packaging. *For the hand-made paper
enthusiast, a visit to the factory
in Worli is a must.*

⑥Bombay Paperie

www.bombaypaperie.com

59 Bombay Samachar Marg,
Fort (opp the Bombay Stock
Exchange).
Ph: 6635 8171, 6635 8172
Mon to Sat 10.30am - 6pm.

Winner of a heritage
award, this stylish store
on the mezzanine
floor of an historic building
is dedicated to keeping the
17th-century tradition of
paper-making by hand alive
in India. A beautiful range
of books, cards, light-fittings
are available as well as a
range of workshops for
children and adults.

*Bombay Paperie supports a wide
range of NGOs via training and
fundraising.*

*There are over
70 markets and
bazaars in Mumbai
selling everything
imaginable –
they are great
to explore.*

Recommended are:

Markets

TOURIST

① Colaba Street Market

The Causeway, Colaba.
Daily 11am - late.

THE hot-spot for tourists. On the crowded pavements are hippie clothing, Kholapuri sandals, Tantra T-shirts, books, magazine, luggage, in fact everything you can imagine. *This is as close as you are going to get to the flea markets of Goa. Negotiate hard.*

PRODUCE

⑪ Crawford Market

Lokmanya Tilka Marg &
Dr Dadabhai Naoroji Rd, Kalbadevi.

The fresh-produce market in an historic building. Also good for tableware Details *(pg78)*.

TRADITIONAL

⑪ Kalbadevi Markets

Cross the road north of Crawford Market to wander the streets of Kalbadevi and Bhuleshwar markets. *These are the traditional markets where temple statues, temple flowers and ceremonial items can be purchased.*

Interesting and very crowded. Around 11am is a good time to arrive.

REAL - LUNGIS TO LUGGAGE...

⏰ Null Bazaar

This market area has a little bit of everything and is a pleasure to stroll around. Start at:

Bombay Lungi Market

"Abba" Bldg, 35 SVP Rd.
Tel: 2346 1008
Daily 9am - noon, 3pm - 9pm.

Has been on the corner since 1942 selling wonderful Madras *lungis*.

Then wander the laneways past produce, meat, flowers, to household items including the great chai carriers, tote bags and wonderful glass bangles.

Universal Luggage

20 SVP Patel Rd.
Tel: 2346 1008
Daily 9.30am - 1.30pm, 2.30am - 8.30pm.

Selling steel trunks for over 65 years (the hand-painted ones are splendid).

FLOWERS

⏰ Bhuleshwar Flower Market

A traditional, but small, market for flowers in this busy area. Note, Hindus believe that touching or smelling the flowers ruins them, so just look, or buy.

ANTIQUES

⏰ Chor Bazaar

Mutton St, Kalbadevi. Sat to Thurs 11am - 7pm.

Known as the *'Thieves Market'* and detailed in the antiques section of this chapter *(pg 70)*. Noon is a good time to arrive, after the stores are set-up and before the crowds. On Fridays many of the stores are shut for the footpath flea market.

FISH

⏰ Sassoon Dock

Colaba.

A great early-morning experience to see the Koli fishermen unload their catch at the dock. The women, in traditional dress, then clean the fish and take the catch in baskets to smaller markets. *Visually a feast, very smelly and no photography allowed.*

FABRIC

⏰ Mangaldas Market

Kalbadevi.
Mon to Sat 1pm - 7pm.

A bustling, busy undercover market that has every kind of fabric at bargain prices — if you are ready to bargain! Popular with fashion designers and housewives.

JEWELLERY

⏰ Zaveri Bazaar

Kalbadevi.
Mon to Sat 11am - 7pm.

A narrow, cluttered and heaving street lined with jewellers; very close to the Mumbadevi temple, whence Mumbai takes it name. A short stroll to Silver Market.

Notes

IVa GORGEOUS
SoBo Pampering:

The most glamorous
city in India, Mumbai
is home to the country's
most beautiful people, as
evidenced by Aishwarya
Rai and her husband
Abhishek Bachchan.

The Bollywood whirl
and capers of the
commercial tycoons make
for the most vibrant
'page-three' culture in the
country. Reports of the
party scene are of utmost
importance even to those
who deny all interest!
Looking good
is an obsession for many
Mumbaikars, making
for an abundant choice
of places to be pampered
and preened.

In addition, the frenetic
pace of life in Mumbai
has created a booming
business in day spas and
relaxation services.

NoBo Pampering:
(pg93)

Looking Good & Feeling Good

Looking Good & Feeling Good

SPA

① Taj Spa

www.tajhotels.com/TajSpa/TajSpamews,Mumbai

Taj Wellington Mews, Luxury Residences,
33 Nathalal Parekh Marg, (opp MSLTA Ground).
Ph: 6657 4401
Weekdays 8am - 9pm, weekends 9am - 9pm.

This urban spa is the most modern and high-end in SoBo. Despite its bland décor, the Taj Spa features a rich range of Indian therapies and has a strong Ayurvedic offering.

A full range of massages, scrubs, wraps, baths, facials, manicures and pedicures are available by experienced therapists. Treatments begin with a rose petal foot wash. Then the traditional neem wood table is cleansed with tended coconut water to create positive energy, followed by the chanting of prayers to evoke healing.

Try the Pranam spa package: a consultation with an Ayurvedic physician, one-on-one yoga class, an ancient ventoz (cupping) treatment, and an Ayurvedic facial.

⑩ Rudra

2nd and 3rd floor, Kwality House,
Kemps Corner (above Amara).
Ph: 2387 2530, 2387 5909
Daily 8am - 11pm. Reservations essential.

Rudra is located in a lovingly restored space at the top of a building in Kemps Corner. It is a rustic, welcoming place with a Jacuzzi on its outdoor terrace. It opened in 2006 as a club offering unlimited services to members. With over 350 members (mainly women, a third men), Rudra is very popular.

The two-hour Rudra Ananda treatment comprises a honey and coconut scrub, to exfoliate and moisturise, followed by a massage utilising traditional Ayurvedic and Tibetan techniques. The Lomi Lomi massage by the Balinese therapists comes highly recommended.

Ayurveda

An ancient traditional system of medicine, Ayurveda is the world's oldest system of health care, practiced in India for over 5,000 years.

The word Ayurveda, meaning 'science of life,' is derived from the Sanskrit words 'ayur' (life) and 'veda' (knowledge or science). Ayurveda is taken very seriously in India, as it is a true medical practice.

Treatments are said to reduce stress, improve circulation, relax tight muscles and rejuvenate the mind and body by eliminating impurities.

⑦ Kerala Ayurvedic Health Spa

www.keralavaidyashala.com

Shop No 1, Neelkanth Bldg, 98 Marine Drive,
Marine Lines (next to Parsi Gymkhana).
Ph: 2288 1508, 2288 3210
Daily 8am - 8pm.

Begun in 1997, KAHS now has seven
branches across Mumbai offering authentic
Ayurvedic therapies. This is a no-frills
experience and not for those in the mood for
luxury. The facility is small (only two treatment rooms) and basic – as is the price at
Rs.900 for a 60 min treatment.

Seated on a wooden table, Ayurvedic powder
is mixed in your hair and luscious warm oil is
applied by two therapists working in tandem.

Being completely naked for a treatment
with no discreet towels and wraps may take
some adjustment, but you are made to feel
completely comfortable. After the massage,
one of the therapists gives you a warm
shower. The experience is like being a child
again – stepping into the world fresh and
full of wonder.

The ① Oberoi Hotel and the ① Taj
Mahal Palace and Tower Hotel
both have excellent spas, big on luxury and
cost, but are open only to hotel guests.

TRADITIONAL SALON

① Touch of Joy

Allana Marg, Colaba (opp Electric House, the street
runs off Colaba Causeway, turn left before Addidas).
Ph: 2204 5566, 2287 5993 Daily 10.30am - 7.30pm.

A good local salon in an old Colaba mansion
full of Mumbai *'ladies who lunch'* having the
works. Touch of Joy is a bustling, down-to-
earth place. *Good value.*

Champi Wallah

A traditional Indian head massage, or champi, is a 'must-do'. This ancient therapy has been lovingly practised in Indian homes for thousands of years. The benefits are evidenced by Indian women's beautiful, shiny, thick hair.

Champi is said to promote hair growth, impart clarity of mind and bring a sense of joy.

Mumbaikars hotly dispute who is the best Champi Wallah. I recommend Shafiq, who has been at the Taj Salon for over 30 years and whose hands will transport you away from all stress and tension. Truly fantastic! Clifford, who has been at Silhouette for over 15 years, does a great head massage.

Head Massage

TRADITIONAL SALON (CONT'D)

❶Taj Salon

The Taj Mahal Palace & Tower, Apollo Bunder, Colaba.
Ph: 6665 3366
Mon to Sat 9am - 7.30pm,
Sun 9.30am - 5.30pm.

The Taj salon is the full service centre for the Who's Who of Mumbai, men and women, visitors and locals alike. The salon, located in the basement of the Taj Palace, offers a comprehensive range of hair treatments, plus manicures, pedicures, waxing, and the Indian art of threading. Ask for Devyani, who is a pro at threading, fast and relatively painless. Kailash does a great pedicure. *You can have your hair, mani and pedi done concurrently… fast and fabulous! The main attraction of the Taj salon is a confident, seasoned staff.*

❸Silhouette Hair & Beauty Salon & Barber Shop

Mezzanine floor
(one level below the pool),
Hilton Towers, Nariman Point.
Ph: 6632 4343
Mon to Sat 9.30am - 7pm,
Sun 10am - 6pm.

Like the Taj Salon, Silhouette offers a full service menu and is popular with glamorous Bombay belles (and blokes).

WORKOUT

⑤ Qi Lifecare

First Floor, West Wing, Eros
Cinema Bldg, Churchgate.
Ph: 6639 0011, 6639 0182
Mon to Sat 6am - 11pm,
Sun 10am - 6pm.

A professional state-of-the-art gym. Light, spacious and immaculately clean (carry your workout shoes as street shoes not allowed in the facility).

Excellent kick-boxing classes and one of the few places in the city to offer spinning.

⑩ Gold's Gym
www.goldsgymindia.com

Garden View, J.Mehta Marg,
Napean Sea Rd, Kemps Corner.
Ph: 2367 9392, 2361 8534
Mon to Sat 6am - 10.30pm,
Sun 9am - 8pm.

A branch of the internationally acclaimed Gold's Gym from Venice Beach, California, the Napean Sea branch is a huge high-energy place to work out. Innovative classes include aerobics, spinning and even pole dancing! Moshe's Café at the gym entrance is a good place to grab a juice and a snack. Other branches at Worli and Bandra.

CONTEMPORARY SALON

⑧ b:blunt

Ground Floor, Block No 1, Kohinoor Bldg,
29 Hughes Rd (coming from Chowpatty, pass
Babunath Temple on your left and turn at the signal.
b:blunt is on the right side corner), Chowpatty.
Ph: 6598 0301, 6598 0370
Tues to Sun 11am - 8pm.
Appointments recommended.

Adhuna Akhtar came to India on a holiday from the UK and luckily for us, she never went back. Working with her brother Osh, she has created a super-modern and stylish concept in hair, *b:blunt*. The name came from her best friend's favourite cocktail and it was a perfect fit for her *'tell it like it is'* attitude when it comes to hair. Adhuna has over 24 years of experience, her team is highly-trained and the focus is 100% hair.

The western-style salon has a Keratase hair spa with services that are like facials for your hair. Come for a good view of hip urban Mumbaikars, both men and women. Good celeb spotting potential, too.

Note: NoBo Branch located at 1st floor, Sundeep
Building, Plot no52, Jai Hind Society, 10th Rd,
JVPD Scheme.

We recommend you support organisations that are socially and/or environmentally sustainable, identified here with the Conscious Travel symbol (pg149)

Mumbai is a good Indian city for running. The route along Marine Drive from Nariman Point to Malabar Hill along the Arabian Sea is one of the world's most scenic runs.

Also recommended are Colaba Woods and Mount Mary Basilica slopes in Bandra.

Beware the heat, humidity, crowds and pollution – it is best to start early. The Standard Chartered Marathon made its debut in January 2004 and continues to increase in stature and participation.

RUN

Bombay Hash House Harriers
www.bombayhash.com
bombayhash@yahoo.com
Ph: 98214 31566 (Call Ketki between 10am - 10pm).

The Bombay Hash arrange monthly runs, moonlight runs and out of town weekends. They run (or walk) on the last Sun of the month, starting at 10am and wrapping up 90 mins later with a drink and snack (beer usually plays an integral part). Hashers meet at the arranged spot, which may be in the heart of the city or might be several hours away. Recent venues have included New Bombay, Elephanta caves, Malabar Hill, Bandra and Thane.

The *'hashers'* are a friendly crowd hailing from many countries and have a wide diversity of occupations in corporate, diplomatic, educational and NGO realms.

SAIL

Mumbai has 70 kilometres of coastline, and increasingly people are taking to the water. The sailing season begins mid-November and lasts until mid-May. Every weekend there are races and there are several major regattas during the sailing season.

There are three active civilian sailing clubs in Mumbai. The most famous, with a rich heritage, is the **Royal Bombay Yacht Club (RBYC)**. A much-loved institution, it accepts guest members from reciprocal clubs. Contact the sailing supervisor, Rajan, with queries at rbycsailing@gmail.com or Ph: 2202 1880, 6752 7200.

The most popular club is the **Colaba Sailing Club (CSC)**. It also has the largest fleet, comprising Seabirds, Lightnings, 420's and Optimists. Visit the CSC website for contact information: www.colabasailingclub.com.

The **Bombay Sailing Association (BSA)** is located in Mandwa, Alibaug. The secretary can be reached on Mobile: 98200 85856.

YOGA

⑦ Kaivalyadhama
www.kdham.com

43, Netaji Subhash Rd, Marine Drive, Marine Lines (next to aquarium).
Ph: 2281 8417, 2288 6256
Mon to Sat 6.30am - 10.30am, 3.30pm - 7pm.

This yogic health centre is the most authentic and prestigious institution for yoga in the city. A medical consultation is required to attend. Monthly membership fees are less than a single class in most western countries!

Bihar Yoga. Whilst there is no ashram in Mumbai, there is an active programme of classes and a full programme of events. For details contact Saranaysi Ramnavmi on Mobile: 98211 22038 between noon-4pm or 7.30pm-9pm.

⑯ **Iyengar Yoga.** If you are an experienced Iyengar practitioner, you can join a class at the Iyengar Yogashraya centre in Lower Parel. Beginners must enrol in a month-long programme. Ph: 2494 8416. Daily 7am - 8pm.

PRODUCTS

⑩ Forest Essentials
www.forestessentialsindia.com

12 Tirupati Apts, Bhulabhai Desai Rd, Kemps Corner.
Ph: 2351 1456
Mon to Sat 10.30am - 8.30pm.

This is a serene shop selling natural beauty, hair, and spa products based on Ayurveda. All are hand-manufactured in small villages in the Himalayas and are gorgeous to use and beautifully packaged for gifts.

Kama Ayurveda is another excellent range of Indian natural products stylishly designed. They are available at **Good Earth (pg47)**, and the spa at the Oberoi Hotel. A full listing is available on their website **www.kamaayurveda.com**

Khadi is the simple and pure range of skin-care products available at the **Khadi Emporium (pg60)** in South Mumbai and **Dhoop (pg48)**, in North Mumbai. *A personal favourite.*

LAUGHTER YOGA

Dr. Kataria's School of Laughter Yoga

www.laughteryoga.org
email: laugh@laughteryoga.org

Ph: 2631 6426
Daily 6.30am or 7am.
Call to confirm time & location.

Speaking to Dr Madan Kataria is a joy, his infectious enthusiasm and belief in Laughter Yoga explains how, in a little over ten years, over 5,000 laughter clubs exist world-wide. When in his home-town, Mumbai, he will be laughing with street kids one morning and corporate high flyers the next.

Clubs meet early morning to breath, stretch, play and of course laugh. These stress-busting sessions are free and open to all people. There are over 85 clubs in Mumbai.

If staying in SoBo, visit the club at the ⑰ **Worli Sea Face**. A large vibrant club with great energy. (Contact Mr Mohit Kapoor on Ph: 2422 8895, 242 26495 or 98200 65119). A smaller club also meets at ❶ **The Gateway** (Contact Mr Girdhar Peshawaria on Ph: 2284 0238 or 98191 23510).

In NoBo, the club that meets near the Otters Club at ②**Joggers Park, Bandra** (W) welcomes visitors, (Contact Mr B.P. Hirani on Ph: 2655 8844 or 93226 75518).

It is best to contact the club and arrange your visit, as this will ensure you have warm attention and guidance, plus you know the exact location and time of the session. Visitors are truly welcome and encouraged to enjoy the benefits of laughter yoga. *So go on, have a great Mumbai experience... 'ha, ha, ho, ho'!*

BEST FUTURE – SHADOW READER

⑫ Anilkumar B. Acharya

Rawal Bldg No 2, Flat No.10, Second Floor,
next to YMCA Bldg, 418 Lamington Rd,
above Punjab National Bank, Opera House Branch,
Opera House, Girgaon.
Ph: 2382 1916, 2382 6988 Daily 9am - 4pm.

On Mr Acharyas' business card, he describes himself as a *'Fortune Teller of Three Births'* from the Ancient Books of Surya Samhita, Bhrugu, Chandra, Shikra, Chhya Shastra and Vaastu Shastri. He believes that *'your shadow can predict your whole life'* based on the principle that the sun's energies affect our existence.

He is a tenth-generation shadow reader from a well-known Chhayashatri Mumbai family. They begin the study at the age of three and by their late 20s become masters. This practice dates back to the early Aryans who worshipped the sun. The shadow-reading takes place standing on the building roof, where three postures are measured. Back in the office, a brief conversation about the date, time and place of birth enables the books to be consulted, the calculations, and the mysteries to unfold.

The reading is an intense session and looks at your life in five- to ten- year periods in detail. Fascinating. Rs.1,500.

Other consultations can be had Tues, Thurs and Sat 5 - 8pm in Andheri. Call for details.

IVb GORGEOUS
NoBo Pampering:

*NoBo is the home
of Bollywood, the film
and television epicentre
of India.*

*The stars, both male
and female, have
rigorous beauty and
fitness régimes, hence
there is an abundance
of great places to look
and feel good.*

Looking Good & Feeling Good

SoBo Pampering:
(pg85)

Looking Good & Feeling Good

WELLNESS

Clay
www.clayindia.com

20/C, Pali Village,
opp P. J. Club, Bandra (W).
Ph: 6581 2444, 6581 2555
Mon to Sat 7.30am - 9pm.

Clay is an integrated wellness centre offering a range of workout options and holistic therapies. Started by Bandra resident and fashion designer Anita Dongre, the space is tranquil and stylish. Classes include yoga, Bums and Tums, Tone & Sculpt, Bollywood Dancing and Salsa. A naturopath and a nutritionist are on staff. Massage treatments include Thai, Swedish, shiatsu and aromatherapy, plus reflexology. My Thai Massage with Falguni, the centre head, was a transformative and special session. *I simply cannot recommend this place highly enough.*

SPA

Sva
www.svaspasalon.com

Gauri Kunj, Kishore Kumar Ganguly Marg,
Juhu Tara Rd, Juhu.
Ph: 2660 7326, 2660 7328, 2660 7368
Daily 11am - 9pm.

Located in a charming Juhu bungalow, Sva is a serious med-spa-salon with a full end-to-end service seamlessly delivered. Come here to be nurtured, rejuvenated and restored. Custom packages begin with a body therapy followed by a facial and then finishing beauty touches. *Geeta has succeeded in gaining a loyal clientele through word-of-mouth. A unique and truly personal service.*

Quan
JW Marriot, Juhu Tara Rd, Juhu.
Ph: 6693 3000
Daily 10am - 10.30pm.

An impressive spa created around the concept of water as the essence of life. The Indian Ayurvedic rooms are beautiful and the couple's room is seriously sensual and sexy. It includes a day-bed for relaxation, a freestanding bath and a mini-bar stocked with champagne and other treats.

Kerala Ayurvedic Health Spa
Sun 'N' Sand Hotel, 39 Juhu Beach, Juhu.
Ph: 6702 4043, 5693 888

Another branch of KAHS *(see pg87)*.

TRADITIONAL SALON

Nalini & Yasmin
www.nalini.in

Sagar Fortune, 201/ 202, 2nd Floor,
Waterfield Rd, Bandra (W).
Ph: 6698 2614, 6698 2615
Daily 11am - 7pm.

So popular is this salon that Colaba gals drive 90 mins each way to have their tresses treated. Stylish mavens from around India have been known to fly in for an appointment. This is serious business: crowded, noisy, buzzy and dedicated to making Indian women as glamorous as possible. Other branches in Juhu and Andheri.

CONTEMPORARY SALON

Christiaan Georgio

Grand Hyatt, off Western Express
Highway, Santacruz (E).
Ph: 6676 1216
Tues to Sun 11am - 8pm.

The sexiest and most luxurious-looking salon
in Mumbai designed by Christiaan himself.
Sassoon-trained and experienced across Asia
(his feats include styling Madonna and Tom
Cruise), he is fanatical about hair. The
salon offers manicures, pedicures and La
Prairie facials.

Mad or Wot

Sai Pooja, Shop No 1, 16th Rd, Bandra (W).
Ph: 6529 0288, 6529 0289
Mon to Sat 11am - 8pm.

*Funky, fun and super fashionable. This salon has
the best energy in the city as well as the best visiting
cards.* Owner Sapna is a Bandra gal and a
true citizen of the world. Trained as a visual
artist, she loves hair, has a hip and loyal
clientele and does a lot of television, film
and fashion work.

YOGA

Yoga Institute

www.yogainstitute.org

Prabhat Colony, Yogendra Marg, Santa Cruz, (E).
Ph: 2611 0506, 2612 2185
Mon to Frid 6.30am - 6.30pm.

*This is the oldest organised yoga institute in the
world, founded in 1918 by Shri Yogendra as a
research and educational organisation.* Today is
directed by his son Jayadeva Yogendra Ph.D.,
who maintains the institution's simplicity,
sincerity and non-commercial nature. It is an
oasis of calm, set on a one-acre block that is
a mini-botanical garden. More than 1,000
people come to the centre daily. Classes begin
at 6.30am. There is also a full offering of
special programmes, longer weekend classes,
workshops and teacher training courses. Note:
Clay *(pg95)* has a great yoga programme.

GOLF

The strictly members-only
Willingdon Club is the most
prestigious club in Mumbai.
The Defence Services'
US Club offers a stunning
sea view and is also
members-only.

Bombay Presidency Golf Club

Dr. Choitram Gidwani Rd,
Chembur.
Ph: 2520 5874, 2520 5875
Tues to Sun 6am - 3.30pm.
(Last tee time 3.30pm).

Established in 1927 and
located an hour away from
the airport, this club is a
favourite among corporates.
Green fees are Rs.1,350
on weekends and Rs.790
on weekdays.

INTERNATIONAL AIRPORT SPA, GYM & POOL

Club Prana

Hyatt Regency Mumbai,
Sahar Airport Rd.
Ph: 6696 1234
Daily 6am - midnight.
Treatments from
9am - 10.15pm.

The spa offers a full range
of massage therapies,
Thalgo facials and beauty
treatments in a soothing
environment. *The outdoor pool
is the best on offer of the airport
hotels.* Guest usage of the
gym, pool, sauna and steam
costs Rs.550.

Notes

V ADVENTUROUS
Discovering:

Getting to know Mumbai could take a lifetime.

It is useful to get help to navigate your way through the city and begin to understand what makes it tick. Here are some excellent trail-finders who offer valuable insight into every aspect of Mumbai life from Slums to Socialites.

Mumbai is India's entertainment capital and there is much to enjoy, at any time day or night, and in any season. Attending a performance, watching a game or seeing a Bollywood film are fast ways of meeting locals and becoming part of their city. Enjoy!

Elite Guides

22 Monica Chudasama Vaziralli

monicavaziralli@hotmail.com

A2, Padamsee Apts,
22-29 Union Park, Khar.
Ph: 2648 2250, 2649 8547.
Mobile: 98200 78611

Monica can trace her lineage to ancestral royalty and is a true Mumbaikar having lived in this city all of her life. *Today, Monica is regarded as the Ambassador of the city and has showcased it to many visiting dignitaries.*

Monica is an interior designer by trade and a society linchpin by design. Beautiful and charming, she knows everyone in the city and is wired into everything going on. Her knowledge covers the glitz of the fashion and film world, high culture and the serious business of shopping

Interested in antiques, jewellery, textiles, fashion or carpets – well in fact anything, Monica can guide you to the best place and ensure you get the best price. *A day with her may well end up at the best party in town or at an exclusive dinner party.* A wonderful insight into elite Mumbai. Her daily charge is approx Rs.22,000.

10 Private Gateway

anees@bom3.vsnl.net.in
rashidaanees@hotmail.com

A8, Sai Manzil,
Altamount Rd, Kemps Corner.
Ph: 2352 5440, 2353 4642,
Mobile: 98202 28255

Rashida Anees has over ten years experience in creating memorable and highly personalized tours for visitors to Mumbai. Born and bred in Mumbai, Rashida went on to travel the world before settling back into her favourite city. A day with Rashida is like joining the elite social set of Mumbai, and she is happy to invite you into the unique world of private clubs and members only experiences.

Indeed, you are given a true insider's view of the city and may even be invited to her gracious home for a delicious lunch. Her passion and profession in interior design makes her an ideal shopping guide and she can arrange visits to many private homes to enjoy the unique aesthetic sensibilities of this city.

If you are interested in learning more about Indian Cuisine, Rashida will take you to the markets, then arrange a cooking demonstration and lunch. If you want to learn more about the art scene, then a tour of the galleries and wine and cheese with the owners is scheduled. Perhaps sport; watching a game of polo, going for a sail, or playing golf at Mumbai's most prestigious club. Anything is possible. Rashida charges a daily rate of USD$125 per person which includes transport and refreshments.

Rashida has a beautiful private family home, Seahorse, located in the tranquil fishing village of Nargol on the west coast, about three hours north of Mumbai. A relaxing experience, priced at USD$100 per person per day inclusive of all meals.

Exploring

WALKING

⑨ Bombay Heritage Walks (BHW)

www.bombayheritagewalks.com
Info@bombayheritagewalks.com

Navyug Niketan, Ground Floor,
185 Walkeshwar Rd, Teenbatti, Malabar Hill.
Ph: 2369 0992

Founded by city architects, Abha Bahl and Brinda Gaitonde, BHW pioneered walking tours in Mumbai. Since 1999 they have hosted many thousands of people on informative and enjoyable walks and have played an important part in raising awareness of the city's rich heritage.

Presenters with backgrounds in heritage management, ancient Indian culture, history, literature and the arts guide all of the walks.

The Fort tour, which lasts about two-and-a-half hours, is ideal for first-time visitors to the city. The walk introduces the history of Bombay as you stroll from the Gateway, past the Taj Hotel and the Yacht Club, to the Regal Circle and onto Kala Ghoda, the University and finish at the Oval Maidan overlooking the grand High Court and an array of 1930s art deco buildings.

Also on offer are specialist tours to fascinating parts of the city such as the ancient and sacred Banganga Tank, the historic commercial area Ballard Estate, and the charming villages of Khotachiwadi and Bandra.

Private walking tours cost Rs.1,500 (for up to three people) and are customised for an individual or for a small group. A small incremental fee is added per extra person.

⑫ Khotachiwadi Welfare & Heritage Trust

Khotachiwadi is a quaint little cluster of 18th and 19th-century homes belonging to the earliest inhabitants of the city of Mumbai, the East Indians (fisher folks, many converted to Christianity by the Portuguese) and the Pathare Prabhus (tradesmen and craftsman). The Wadi feels like a sleepy coastal village and is only 30 mins from Colaba. *There are some architectural gems and it is a wonderful cultural mélange.*

Born in Khotachiwadi, James Ferraria is a famous Mumbai fashion designer *(pg51)*, and passionate advocate for the area and its preservation, and was instrumental in setting up the Trust.

Visit the 150-year-old *Ferraria family home* which is located at 47-G, Khotachi Wadi, Girgaum. The ladies of the Trust can arrange a delightful afternoon tea, torchlight evening walking tours and can provide a guide for those who are keen to explore this unique area. For details, call 2388 7292 or 2387 5725.

TOURING

Beyond Bombay Tours

beyondbombay@gmail.com

Ph: 98677 64409

Shriti Tyagi, the founder of Beyond Bombay has studied literature, written scripts, acted and edited magazines. She is passionate about Mumbai. She now runs customised tours, including:

Bollywood Tours

Mumbai is the home of Bollywood and one would be forgiven for thinking Bollywood is Mumbai. However despite being the worlds largest film industry with over double the output of Hollywood, there is no tourism offering as of yet, no regular studio visits and no organised tours of the homes of Bollywood stars.

Shriti Tyagi co-founded a theatre group, worked as a director and scriptwriter, has acted, stage-managed and worked on documentaries and films. Using her inside knowledge she has put together a great package.

First, go to a Hindi film together and experience first-hand the adoration of the stars. Then head up to the Prithvi Café *(pg38)* for a snack and some celeb-spotting. On the drive, become immersed in the Cinemascape that Mumbai is, the city itself having been the star of many big Bollywood blockbusters. Finish up at Film City to go on set and see a production.

Make sure to give as much notice as possible for this tour as negotiating entry into the film studios takes time and effort. Tours from US$75.

Bookworming Tours

Mumbai is a character in more books than any other Indian city. Designed for voracious readers these tours bring to life the books and the characters. Take a walk down book lane.

Tours conducted to date include: *Rediscovering Dharavi* by Kalpana Sharma, *Maximum City* by Suketa Mehta and *Shantaram* by Gregory David Roberts. Tours in development include *Ravan* and *Eddie* by Kiran Nagarkar and *Bombay Meri Jaan* by Naresh Fernandes and Jerry Pinto.

Beyond Bombay are open to doing more, name your book and give them time to read it! The customized tours range in price from US$75 to US$200.

Fishing village
Cuffe parade

Mumbai Tours

Mumbai Magic

www.mumbaimagic.com
deepa@mumbaimagic.com

Ph: 98677 07414

Deepa Krishnan is now applying her skills from a high-powered corporate life in banking to her passion for the city. She has created an uber-professional guided tour business that runs set tours and arranges customized tours for high-end clientele. To date she has delivered specialty tours covering everything from antique textiles and artistic brassware, making a living from the sea, tea and coffee rituals to the Indian art scene.

Mumbai Magic has three types of standard tours:

Walking tours for small groups (min of two people) including the Crawford Market and Bhuleshwar Bazaar Walk, the Chor Bazaar walk, the Worli Fishing Villages and a Fort Heritage walk. The walks last for two hours and start at Rs.1,250 per person.

Personalised tours by car, which can be for a half-day or a full-day. Recommended is the *'Peoples of Mumbai'* where you visit the Parsi, Jain, Hindu, Jew, Muslim and Christian communities and places of interest, plus look at a fishing village. The cost ranges from Rs.4,000 to Rs.8,000 per person depending on the length of time and number of people in the group.

Boat tours to Elephanta Island. Accompanied by a knowledgeable guide this tour costs Rs.2,475 per person.

The tours are all conducted by authorative guides in a thoughtful way (including illustrated handouts and a memento gift, plus bottled water and snacks). They are also available in German and Spanish. *Highly recommended.*

TOURING (CONT'D)
Slum Tours

*Krishna Pujari and
Chris Way started the
Reality Tours in 2005
and are sensitive to
the issues of running
a company that may
be accused of being
exploitive.*

*They have pledged
80% of profits after
tax (when they reach
that stage) to NGO's.
Together with Mesco,
they have started
a community and
education centre.*

*They have a completely
transparent company,
the website discloses
all revenue and costs
and tackles head-on
the issues raised in
undertaking these tours.*

① Reality Tours and Travel
www.realitytoursandtravel.com
info@realitytoursandtravel.com

Akber House, First Floor, Nowroji Fardonji Rd, Colaba.
(opp Laxmi Vilas Hotel, just off Colaba Causeway).
Ph: 2283 3872, 24-hour Mobile: 98208 22253
Tours run daily.
Office open: Mon-Frid 10.15am - 6.45pm.
Sat 10.15am - 3.45pm.

Dharavi, Asia's biggest *'slum'*, is described as a place of poverty and hardship but also a place of enterprise, humour and non-stop activity. *These tours are run sensitively with the apparent blessing of the Dharavi residents.*

The tour mainly focuses on commercial areas, with time in the residential areas kept to a minimum; highlights include visiting a school and the attractive pottery. No photography is allowed, nor any gifting, no matter how small. The briefing in the car and on the walk is thorough, interesting, pragmatic and above all, hopeful.

I learnt a lot, was humbled by the industrious activity and warmth of the people we saw and surprised by the well-established building, infrastructure (including a cyber café) and commerce that exist. Dharavi is at the heart of small-scale industry in Mumbai, with an annual turnover of US$665 million. Over half of Mumbai's population lives in slums similar to Dharavi and I finished the tour more informed, more respectful and now think of Dharavi as a village, albeit a large one!

We recommend you support organisations that are socially and/ or ennvironmentally sustainable, identified here with the Conscious Travel symbol (pg149)

CRUISING

Being on the water is one of the best ways to experience Mumbai. Gentle waves and sea breeze, tranquility and calm as you leave the city behind. One can catch a ferry for just a few rupees or, at the other extreme, charter a cruiser. Sailing information *(pg91)*.

By Ferry

One of the true pleasures of Mumbai is to catch one of the gaily-painted ferries from the Gateway of India and head across the sea. The ferries ply between The Gateway and Elephanta Island or across to Alibaug *(pg116)*. They do not operate during the monsoon; at other times, they start from about 9am and run regularly all day until 5.30pm and cost a mere Rs.100.

To get a ticket simply head down to the ferries and the ticket-seller will find you or go to the ferries office in the little row of shacks behind The Gateway. You can call the office to check times, Ph: 2282 0139.

All boats are priced similarly with a small difference between the standard and the luxury ones, the latter coming with padded seats and a store selling soft drinks.

By Luxury Yacht

The Taj Hotel boat operates from October to May. This 50-foot luxury cruiser is richly-appointed with fine leather, fabric and hand finished wood. It has three bedrooms, a dining room, sitting room and upper and lower deck.

You and up to ten friends, can cruise the Mumbai Harbour for two hours at a cost of Rs.48,000. Or have a romantic twilight cruise for two hours, with butler service and beverages included at a cost of Rs.55,000. A journey over to Elephanta, for up to ten people, taking three hours costs Rs.65,000.

A romantic option is to spend the night on board. The Arabian Nights Fantasy cruise includes a sumptuous dinner and breakfast for one or two couples, and costs Rs.195,000.

The yacht is in high demand, so book well ahead by calling the Taj Catering Sales Office on Ph: 6665 3366.

Enjoying

Time Out Mumbai launched in September 2004. The magazine has gone from strength to strength. *It is an essential purchase to tap into the wealth of entertainment options in the city.*

THEATRE, MUSIC & DANCE

Mumbai has over 40 theatres, auditoriums and venues for drama, dance and music. Performances may be in English, Hindi, Marathi or Gujarati.

The most celebrated venues include:.

③ National Centre for the Performing Arts, (NCPA)

www.ncpamumbai.com

NCPA Marg, Nariman Point, next to Oberoi Hotel
Ph: 6622 3737
Box office open daily 9am - 7pm
Café 10am - 10pm.

India's premier performing arts centre is spread over eight acres at Nariman Point, Mumbai's Manhattan. The NCPA is a unique mega-complex, with a host of venues and state-of-the-art facilities. There are five theatres; the largest can seat over 1,000 people and the smallest just 100 people. Of special note are the following:

The Tata Theatre was conceived, designed and built to serve the exacting acoustic and visual requirement of Indian music, dance and related art forms.

The Piramal Art Gallery specialises in exhibiting works of leading Indian and international photographers.

The Jehangir Nicholson Gallery of Modern Art serves as a popular venue for international exhibitions on painting, sculpture and other visual arts.

⑰ Nehru Centre

www.Nehru-centre.org

Dr Annie Besant Rd, Worli.
Ph: 2492 0510 Daily 10am - 6pm.

 The Nehru Centre was conceived in 1972, as a living testament to Jawaharlal Nehru. The Culture Wing, which in particular supports young performing artists, has regular cultural programmes in all branches of performing arts including dance, drama and music.

The Nehru Centre Art Gallery is also dedicated to the promotion of young talent and provides a platform for them to exhibit their work along with that of eminent artists.

The Nehru Planetarium is a centre for scientific study of astronomy; scientists and scholars meet for discussions and lectures. The Planetarium is currently running the 32nd sky theatre programme *'Stars and wonders of the universe';* the English version of the show runs 3pm - 4pm from Tues to Sun.

The Discovery of India Exposition is' a permanent display covering every aspect of artistic, intellectual and philosophical attainment of India through ages.

Prithvi Theatre

www.prithvitheatre.org

20 Janki Kutir, Juhu Church Rd, Vile Parle (W).
Ph: 2614 9546
Tues to Sun. Show times at Prithvi tend
to be 6pm & 9pm (Box office 10am - 1pm)
Café 10am - 11.30pm Book Shop 2pm - 10pm.

Prithvi is THE theatre in the city and has an innovative show on every day (excluding Mondays), and about 400 shows annually. It is an intimate 200-seater with a thrust stage and excellent acoustics. It is a completely non-profit entity depending on the patronage of individuals and companies. Prithvi ticket rates are Rs.50 on Tuesdays and Wednesdays and range between Rs.50 and Rs.200 on other days.

A charming café, a photo gallery and a lovely little bookshop are other attractions at the Prithvi venue.

Prithvi also organise the annual Prithvi Theatre Festival in November, plus popular weekend shows at pretty Horniman Circle Garden on the first weekend of every non-rainy month. Regular show times in the garden are at 8pm.

CULTURAL CENTRES

Asia Society India Centre

www.asiasociety.org.in

12th Floor, Arcadia,
195 NCPA Marg, Nariman Point.
Ph: 6610 0888
Mon to Fri 9am - 5pm.

John D Rockefeller III founded the Asia Society in 1956, in New York. Initially established to promote greater knowledge of Asia in the US, it now includes intra-Asian connections and exchange as part of its mandate. The Mumbai centre provides year-round programming in the areas of business, policy, social issues, arts and culture. Events include lectures, panel discussions and film screenings in diverse topics including: textiles, private equity, new Indian art and climate change.

Alliance Française de Mumbai

www.afindia.org/bombay

40 New Marine Lines,
Theosophy Hall.
Ph: 2203 6187, 2203 5993
Mon to Frid 9.30am - 1pm, 2pm - 5.30pm. Sat 9.30am - 1pm.

A celebration of French culture. The Alliance has a full cultural programme of conferences, film festivals, shows, concerts and exhibitions.

British Council

www.britishcouncil.org/india-regional-mumbai

British Deputy High Commission
Mittal Tower, 'C' Wing, 2nd Floor,
Nariman Point
Ph: 2282 3560
Mon to Frid 9am - 5pm.

Committed to an ongoing cultural exchange between Britain and India, the council conducts a vivid and continuous range of performing, literary and visual arts, events and projects.

Goethe-Institut

www.goethe.de/ins/in/mum

Max Mueller Bhavan, K Dubash Marg, Kala Ghoda.
(next to Jehangir Art Gallery).
Ph: 2202 7542
Mon to Sat 10am - 6pm.

This German cultural centre has a very active programme of exhibitions, film screenings, concerts and other special events.

Make sure to see a Bollywood film at one of these grand dames of cinema: **Eros, Liberty,** or the **Regal**. These art deco cinema halls, are wonderful nostalgic experiences, however are under threat from the developers. **Metro Cinema** has been renovated, keeping the heritage exterior but eradicating the beauty of the interior.

Good to know that few Hindi films have English subtitles and many last three hours or longer! Full movie screenings are listed in daily newspapers and 'Time Out' magazine.

The Eros Cinema

CINEMA

Mumbai has hundreds of cinemas. Traditionally these were single screen halls showing the latest film from Bollywood. In the last decade, the multiplex is taking over and many old theatres are closing.

⑤EROS CINEMA
Churchgate
Ph: 2282 2335

⑦LIBERTY CINEMA
Marine Lines
(nr Bombay Hospital)
Ph: 2203 1196

①REGAL CINEMA
S.P Nukherji Chowk, Colaba
Ph: 2202 1017

⑦METRO CINEMA
Marine Lines (next to Liberty Cinema)
Ph: 2403 6474

③ INOX

www.inoxmovies.com

2nd Floor, Cross Rd 2, opp Bajaj Bhavan, Nariman Pt.
Ph: 6659 5959

The INOX multiplex was the first and remains the only multiplex in SoBo. It has five state-of-the-art auditoriums screening a wide variety of international and Indian films. Worth paying a few rupees extra for the more spacious leather seats in Royale Class.

SPECTATOR SPORTS

Horse Racing

④ Royal Western India Turf Club

www.rwitc.com

Race Course, Mahalaxmi.
Ph: 2307 1401, 2307 1407, 2307 1438

The Royal Western India Turf Club is the premier racing Club in India and is often referred to as the 'Ascot of the East'. The club extends temporary memberships to visitors (contact the secretary).

The Mumbai racing season begins in mid-November and ends in April with racing mostly on Thur and Sun. During this period, there are 55 days of racing with total horse strength of approximately 1,500. *The Indian Derby day,* held on the first Sunday of February, is the most glamorous event where well-heeled locals enjoy champagne and cucumber sandwiches.

During the monsoon season, from July to October, racing is conducted at Pune, which also has a very pretty racetrack.

Cricket

Mumbai is the cricket capital of India and it seems that all of Mumbai is playing cricket all of the time, whether in small laneways or world-class stadiums. By far the most charming matches to watch are the informal ones, played on the picturesque maidans in the Fort area.

⑤ Mumbai Cricket Association

Wankhede Stadium,
D. Rd, Churchgate.
Ph: 2281 1795, 2281 7876, 2281 9910

The MCA, established in 1930, has produced 50 players who have played tests for India, including the famous Vijay Merchant, Sunil Gavaskar and Sachin Tendulkar.

Bombay hosted the first-ever Test Match in India, in 1933-34 against England. After WWII, the Cricket Club of India's Brabourne Stadium was home to the MCA until the 45,000-capacity Wankhede Stadium, was built in 1975. It regularly hosts test matches, one-day internationals and other first-class matches during the season September to April.

Notes

VI WILDLY ADVENTUROUS
Escaping:

*In this section find
the seven best 'Escapes'
from Mumbai.*

*Travel by boat, car,
train and plane to
enjoy some of the best
experiences in India.*

Escape

GOA

Where to stay

Panchavatti Guest House Retreat

www.islaingoa.com

Corjuem Island, Aldona, Bardez.
Ph: 98225 80632

I simply cannot imagine a better place to relax and enjoy Goa. Isla 'Loulou' Van Damme has created the perfect retreat. The 24-acre property has magnificent views overlooking the Mapusa River, paddy-fields and hills. Her stylish home has four guest rooms; the spacious writer's room was my favourite. Meals are a delight, with excellent fresh cuisine, and are served privately or at the table d'hôte with other (always interesting) guests. The daily rate is Rs.8,000 (Rs.9,000 in Dec/Jan) for two guests per room, inclusive of all meals.

Apart from relaxing by the stunning pool, there are lovely walks through the countryside on the island; Loulou knows Goa intimately and can recommend interesting adventures ranging from the best antique shop in Goa to a gourmet beach shack. Loulou does yoga every morning and guests are welcome to join her. An Ayurvedic doctor is available for consultations on request, as are two excellent, highly-trained masseurs, who specialise in traditional Kerala Massage.

Loulou's is about 75 mins from the airport. The nearest town is Mapusa, and the beaches of Calangute, Baga, Anjuna and Vagator are a 30 min drive away. The northern beaches of Morjim, Mandrem and Arambol are 45 mins away.

Other places to stay:

Nilaya Hermitage
www.nilaya.com
Arpora.
Ph: 0832 227 6793
Rich Hippie Scene
US$430 per night,
minimum of
three nights.

Raman
Calangute.
Ph: 98221 80133,
0832 227 7797
Quality Beach
Cottages. Rs.4,500.
Dome Room best.

Elsewhere
www.aseascape.com
Mandrem.
Ph: 98200 37387
Private Luxury.
(Angelina and Brad
stayed here). Lux tents
start at US$400 per
week, houses start at
US$1,700 per week.

Goa Beach

Delicious – Where to eat

Lila Café
www.lilacafegoa.com

nr Baga-River, Arpora-Baga and Bardez.
Ph: 0832 2279843.
9am - 6pm. Closed Tuesday.

This open-air picturesque café is THE meeting place in Goa. On weekends, everyone meets here to catch up on the night before and make plans for the day ahead. Enjoy all-day breakfasts, good pumpernickel sandwiches and espresso coffee.

La Plage
Answem Beach, between Morjim and Arambol
Mobile: 98221 21712
8.30am - 10pm.

This is the Goa of the imagination, a stylish, hip café run by a French couple, right on the beach serving great food and chilled wine. Note: simple huts available to stay in. Sister restaurant to Le Restaurant Française in Calangute.

Best Experience

The real question here, is what, if anything, is worth leaving the comfort of Loulou's place for. These are:

Ingo's Saturday Night Bazaar
Arpora.
Sat 6pm-midnight.

A Goa institution. Enjoy meandering around the stalls, mingling with all of Goa: original hippies, rich hippies, backpackers, package tourists and locals.

Sunday Mass
Simply head to the nearest Portuguese church and join in for the Sunday service. A beautiful Goan moment.

Fort Tiracol
www.nilaya.com

Tiracol.
Ph: 02366 227 631

Take a picturesque drive north through Goan villages and the beaches of Morjim, Ashvem and Arambol, then catch the ferry to Tiracol. The Portuguese fortress, overlooking the Arabian Sea and the Tiracol River, is now a boutique hotel. The terrace is unbeatable for a long, lazy lunch. Boat trips for dolphin viewing can be arranged. Reservations essential. *If staying choose the room called Friday.*

GOA (CONT'D)

Fabulous – What to buy

Edwin Pinto Shoes

www.janotagoa.com

Janota, Adleia Aurino, nr Damian de Goa,
Povorim, Bardez.
Ph: 0832 241 2129
Mobile: 98504 60578
Mon - Sat 9am - 1pm,
2.30pm - 6pm.
Also, Arpora Market (Ingos),
on Sat nights.

Soft leather chappals for men and women, hand-made in rich colours and distinctive designs with a touch of whimsy.

Literati Bookshop and Café

E/1-282, Gaura Vaddo,
Calangute, Bardez
(next to La Fenice Restaurant).
Phone 0832 227 7740
10am - 7pm, closed Wed.

Located in a pretty bungalow set in a garden, this is a little bookstore and café. There is a good selection of local authors and it is the best bookshop in Goa.

Sangolda

E2-6, Chogm Rd, Sangolda, Bardez.
Ph: 0832 240 9310
Mon-Sat 10am - 6.30pm.

Housed in a rambling bungalow this is a stylish and sexy store featuring ethnic and colonial furniture, brass & copper vessels, linens, wood and glass objects. A *"must-do"* and nestled amongst a group of other interesting shops.

Sosa's

E 245, Rua de Ourem, Panjim.
Ph: 0832 222 8063
10am - 7pm. Closed Sunday.

A sexy fashion boutique in an historic Fountainhauz building with beautiful tiled floors. Contemporary Indian fashion for men and women including a great range of Goa's hippest, and extremely talented designer, Savio Jon.

How to get there

Easily reached from Mumbai via domestic airlines and has an international airport.

Getting Around

Taxis are abundant and can be taken for short hops. However, better value and more convenient is to simply hire a car for the day, approx Rs.1,000 depending on kilometres travelled. Scooter taxis can be fun!

Book

Reflected in Water: Writings on Goa (essays, poems, stories and extracts) edited by Jerry Pinto includes great local writers, Teotonia R. de Souza, Frederick Noronha, Frank Simoes and outsiders including Graham Greene and William Dalrymple. Also recommended is *Ferry Crossings: Short stories from Goa* edited by Manohar Shetty.

Heritage

AHMEDABAD

Ahmedabad is a thriving commercial centre in Gujarat. It is one of the most interesting destinations in India. Founded in 1411, the old walled town contains fine Indian Islamic monuments, exquisite Hindu and Jain temples and wonderful carved wooden Havelis.

Once called the Manchester of East, it remains a leading centre of the textile industry. The prosperous city welcomed inspiration from external sources, including Corbusier and Eames and is now famous for its modern architecture and design. Also known for its educational institutions like the IIM for management, NID for design, CEPT for town planning and architecture, MICA for communications and NIFT for fashion design.

Mahatma Gandhi developed his ideas and principles at his home, the Satyagraha Ashram, which became the nerve centre of India's freedom movement. *Ahmedabad enjoys a vibrant cultural life and has some spectacular festivals throughout the year, with the annual Kite festival in January being the highlight.*

Where to stay

The House of MG

www.houseofmg.com

Opp. Sidi Saiyad Mosque, Lal Darwaja.
Ph: 079 2550 6946

One of my favourite hotels in India. Located in heritage property this twelve-roomed boutique hotel is stylish and intimate. Owned and sensitively managed by Abhay Mangaldas, staying here enables you to tap into everything on offer in the city. The staff is knowledgeable and the experience is full, including some of the best food and the best shopping in town. The rooms are a perfect blend of traditional design with contemporary facilities. My favourite rooms are the verandah suites with a traditional *jhoola* (swing).

Arts Reverie

www.artsreverie.com

1824 Khijda Sheri,
opp Jain Derasar, Dhal Ni Pol,
Astodia Gate
Ph: 079 3252 1926
Mobile: 098923 31257

This charming 1920s house set in a heritage enclave is a guesthouse for creative arts professionals. Guests find a creative environment in which to pursue their art, the simple chic rooms come with work spaces. Cultural tours can be arranged.

Best Experience

Calico Textile Museum

This is the premier textile museum of the country, and one of the most celebrated institutions of its kind in the world. The collection contains rare, exquisite fabrics from across in India, dating back to the 17th-century. Morning tours begin at 10.30am and cover the textiles; afternoon tours commence at 2.45pm and cover the Sarabhai foundation collection of artifacts. Closed Wednesdays and Public Holidays.

Architectural Highlights

See Corbusier's work from the 1950s including the Mill Owners Building, and the Shodhan and Sarabhai houses. The Institute of Management is a fine building by Louis Khan.

Vintage Cars

Ph: 079 2282 0699
Daily 10am - 6pm.

Pranlal Bhogilal, the industrialist from Mumbai, has India's finest collection of fine vintage and classic cars. His *Auto World Museum* is located at his *'farm'*, a 2,200-acre estate, just a 30 min drive from Ahmedabad.

Walk the Walled City

Enjoy a sonic stroll in the old city. Learn about architecture, history and folklore at your own pace, listen to interviews with local figures and famous residents. The *'D-Tours'* MP3 rental is available at The House of MG, Monday through Sunday from 8am -7pm. Start before 9am or after 5pm to avoid the sun and traffic.

AHMEDABAD Best Experience (CONT'D)

Gandhi Ashram

Located on a quiet stretch of the Sabarmati River, Gandhi set up the Ashram in 1915 and it was from here that the Salt March commenced in 1930. The famed architect Charles Correa designed the museum and the hand-made paper factory nearby is worth a visit.

Cultural Performance

www.darpana.com

Ph: 079 2755 1389

Darpana Academy of Performing Arts is at the forefront of new and innovative performing arts work. The season starts at the end of September and runs until June. The Natarani amphitheatre is one of the most spectacular venues in the country with a stage that has the river as the backdrop.

Fabulous – What to buy

The city has wonderful textiles, silver jewellery, hand-made paper and kites. The Ravivari market, dating back to the 15th-century when it was called Khasbazaar, is held every Sunday, late afternoon, underneath the Ellisbridge. Other great shopping includes:

Banascraft

8, Chandan Complex, Swastik Crossroads, C.G. Rd, Navarangpura (nr Mirch Masala Restaurant).
Ph: 079 2640 5784
Daily 10am - 8pm.

An outlet for the non-for-profit SEWA organisation owned and managed by 1,500 women craft artisans of Kutch and Banaskantha. Traditional embroidery with contemporary designed clothing, accessories and homewares.

Gamithiwala Fabrics

Haijra Gate, (nr Badshah's) Manekchowk.
Ph: 079 2214 8879, 079 2214 8104.
Ph: 079 2640 5784
Mon to Sat 11am - 7pm.
Closed for prayers Friday 12.30pm - 2pm.

A wonderful place to buy traditional hand-block-printing using natural dyes.

House of MG Gift Shop

Located near the hotel reception desk. A stylish collection of high quality local craft and vintage pieces. The range includes clothing and accessories, furniture, home décor and gifts.

Art Book Centre

Madalpur (nr Jain Temple), Ellisbridge.
Ph: 079 2658 2130
Daily 10am - 6pm.

A comprehensive collection from Mapin, India's largest art publisher, based in Ahmedabad.

Bandhej

Shri Krishna Centre, nr Mithakali Six Rds, Navarangpura.
Ph: 079 2642 2181
Daily 10am - 8pm.

Founded in Ahmedabad and now across India, a contemporary clothing collection for men and women from natural weaves.

Mati Contemporary Ceramics

5b Jain Society, Ellisbridge.
Ph: 079 2657 8368
Mon - Sat 11am - 7pm.

Charming, simple local pottery since 1980.

Delicious – Where to eat

Agashiye

Daily noon - 3pm, 7pm - 11pm.

Located on the spacious roof top terrace of the House of MG, this is like dining in a contemporary Gujarati home and is held in high esteem by foodies across India. Agashiye serves pure-vegetarian food only and the menu changes daily and as per season.

Note: Alcohol is prohibited throughout Gujarat, however it is possible for foreign nationals and out-of-town visitors to get permits which enable alcohol to be bought at a few hotel shops and consumed in the privacy of your room.

Swati Snacks

Opp Aveh Associated Bldg, Law Garden, Ellisbridge. Ph: 079 2640 2185, 2640 5900
Daily 11.45am - 10.45pm.

Contemporary Gujarati food in a modern setting. Popular with well-to-do locals and ex-pats. Clean, hip, cheap and terrific food. Sister restaurant to Swati in Mumbai, *(pg 23)*.

How to Get There

Ahmedabad is easily reached from Mumbai via domestic airlines and has an international airport. From Mumbai, the road journey is 545km. There are direct flights and overnight trains to Jaipur, an overnight train to Jodhpur, and Udaipur is a five-hour drive on an excellent highway.

Getting Around

Hotels can arrange taxis. A friend discovered Johny, a fabulous English-speaking auto-rickshaw driver who knows the city well. Ph: 982 4361058, 079 2533 2021.

Book

An Autobiography or The story of my experiments with truth (by M. K. Gandhi). Written in 1925 at the Ashram in Ahmedabad.

Fast Get-Away
ALIBAUG

Alibaug to Mumbaikars is the Hamptons to New Yorkers, the Cotswolds to Londoners and Palm Beach to Sydneysiders. This coastal town is a rustic unspoilt getaway for the affluent Bombay crowd. They own farms and bungalows close to the sea shore and enjoy entertaining lavishly at home. Visiting Alibaug is like seeing Goa twenty or thirty years ago. Go soon before tunnels and bridges turn this into an extension of the city; real estate is doubling in price annually, as the inevitable march towards commercialisation takes place.

Where to stay

Ideally, get invited as a houseguest. The hotels lack charm. However, Ahaar is a little gem owned and run by Avnish (a serious yachtie who looks after Mr Mallya's fleet), Abhishek (Bob) and Karan, who both own restaurants and hotels in Mumbai.

Ahaar Guest House
www.kihimvillage.com/ahaar.htm
ahaar@kihimvillage.com

Ph: Rodney 93241 34109 or
Avanish 02141 232 761

The five modern guest rooms are simply and freshly decorated. The tree house on two floors is the only room to have air con and costs Rs.1,500 per night, the other four rooms are Rs.1,250 per night All rooms have attached bath, cable TV, uninterrupted electricity with power backup and Wi-Fi Internet connectivity. Ahaar hosts yoga weekends and artists camps and is popular with the owner's friends from Mumbai. Book early!

Where to eat

The Courtyard at Ahaar offers both Mediterranean and Indian cuisine catered for by Monza and Pritam ka Dhaba restaurants in Mumbai. There is a very well-stocked bar specialising in wine.

Open Friday evenings for dinner, Saturdays for all three meals, and Sundays for brunch with music by Woody, who is a saxophonist, flute player and music producer (ambient, funky lounge and dance styles) from New Zealand. Woody has come to India having been invited by Pandit Hari Prasad Chaurasia to study *Bansuri* (flute) with him at his *Gurukul* in Juhu. Restaurant bookings are handled by Bob on Ph: 98702 87702.

Best Experience

Chill, unwind, relax. Enjoy strolling around the
pretty villages and along the unspoilt beaches.
Kashid Beach 30kms from Alibaug gets
particularly good reviews.

How to Get There

There are three ferry companies, namely,
PNP, Ajanta and Maldar that leave from the
Gateway of India to Mandawa during the
non-monsoon season, every hour from 6am
until 6pm and it is the same for the return
journey.

The trip takes about 45 mins to an hour. Ferry
office at Gateway of India Ph: 022 2282 0139.
During the monsoon the ferries stop working
and keen Alibaug visitors must travel the
130km route by road, taking over three hours.

An alternative faster journey is to go by
speedboat that takes about 25 mins to make
the crossing. Contact Aashim Mongia email
to aashim@vsnl.net or call him at Ph: 98201
30940. He gets very busy, so make sure to
book at least two days prior for a weekend
trip, or the day before for a weekday trip.
The crossing is Rs.5,500 each way.

Getting Around

There are auto rickshaws
and taxis on the island that
are easy to pick up. The
well-heeled locals enjoy
hurtling around in open
topped jeeps.

Book

Selective Memory
(by Shobha Dé).

Shobha has homes in
Mumbai and Alibaug.
Often called India's Jackie
Collins, she is a novelist (14
books) and a columnist in
newspapers and magazines.
After making her name
as a model, she founded
and edited three popular
magazines 'Stardust', 'Society',
and 'Celebrity'.

Meditate
PUNE

Osho International Meditation Resort

www.osho.com

17 Koregaon Park.
Ph: 020 6601 9900

Originally called the Rajneesh Ashram, the spiritual movement was started in 1974 and promoted meditation and uninhibited expression of body and mind. The ashram was quickly associated with free love and became controversial, but has now settled into a sophisticated retreat for those wanting to learn meditation and get re-energised.

The Dalai Lama described this resort as *'A very beautiful place. It is like being in a peaceful forest'.* I was impressed with the tranquil beauty of the 40-acre campus and also the super modern and luxurious facilities including marble pathways, elegant black buildings and an Olympic-sized swimming pool.

Osho is like a spiritual United Nations, over a 100,000 visitors from 100 countries visit the resort annually. Choose your own schedule: rest, swim, have a massage, take a course, meditate – or just be.

You are encouraged to learn simple Osho Active Meditations, techniques specifically designed for the over-charged mind and stress-impacted body. Daily sessions are held from 6am-9pm, and take place in the world's largest meditation hall, the Osho Auditorium.

Where to stay

The Osho Guesthouse was conceived as simply a beautiful place to stay. It is indeed a stylish, serene place. All 60 rooms have double beds, A/C, fresh air supply and attached bathroom. Rs.3,630 per night, (Rs.4,180 per double).

The Sunderban Hotel, next door to Osho, has 50 rooms and is set in a nice garden. Room rates are similar. Ph: 2612 4949.

Welcome Stay

For first-time visitors there is a two-night/three-day package for Rs.9,700 for a single or Rs.14,950 for a couple. This includes accommodation, food, robes, registration and a meditation pass.

One-Day Visit

A one-day page package is available for Rs.1,280. This includes: Entrance, HIV/Aids test, entry card and photos. Register at the Welcome Centre between 9am-3.30pm (closed for lunch, 1pm-2pm). Bring your passport and visa.

Alternatively, a 20 min guided walk-through takes place between 9am-1pm and 2pm-4pm daily, for a small fee (Rs.10).

The AIDS Test

You will need to take an HIV/AIDS test at Osho, as test results from elsewhere are not accepted. This costs Rs.180 and is a rapid HIV I & II laser, finger-prick test taking less than 15 mins. Entry into the resort is dependent on a negative result.

What to Wear

Maroon robes are worn inside the resort. White robes are worn for the evening meditation. Expect to spend roughly Rs.1,600 for four robes (two of each colour).

Delicious – Where to eat

The Osho Resort

The Osho Resort provides low-cost, high-quality vegetarian (mostly organic) cuisine. However, for a change, there are excellent alternatives nearby including:

Malaka Spice

www.malakaspice.com

Vrindavan Aparts, opp Sanas Residency,
North Main Rd, Koregaon Park, Malaka.
Ph 020 2613 6293, 020 2614 1088
Daily 10am - 11pm.

Praful and his wife moved back from S.E. Asia to India with a passion for food, creating Malaka Spice in 1999. This charming indoor, outdoor restaurant has great Asian food, a good wine list plus an active arts programme.

Fabulous – What to buy

The Osho Boutique is full of "ahsram chic", however is open to registered visitors only. The bookshop at the Welcome centre has a comprehensive selection of books, CD's and DVD's and is open to the public.

The street stalls nearby in Koregaon Park are great places to pick up the famous Osho slippers and gaily-decorated Birkenstock inspired chappals.

How to Get There

There are at least six train services daily to and from Mumbai. They take about four hours, details on www.indianrailways.gov. in. Bookings best made through your hotel concierge, or at the foreigners counter at the VT terminal in Mumbai.

Getting Around

Local pre-paid taxis are available at the airport. By far the most common way to get around is the auto-rickshaw, available everywhere!

Book

Above all, don't wobble; Individual Conversations with the Contemporary Mystic (by Osho). Published 1977 & 2006.

My Pune (conceived and jointly published by Elephant Design and The Maharashtra Chamber of Commerce, Industry & Agriculture) in 2006. An insider's guide to living and enjoying the city.

Udaipur has an abundance of palatial properties to choose from and if staying at one, make sure to visit the others for a drink and/ or a meal.

Other Places to Stay

Oberoi Udaivilâs
www.oberoihotels.com

Haridasji Ki Magri, Udaipur.
Tel: 0294 2433300

Rated the 'Best Hotel in the World' in the 2007 Readers Poll in Travel+Leisure Magazine. Udaivilas, located on the banks of Lake Pichola looks across to the palaces. The 100 rooms and suites have palatial architecture and there is a fine spa. Udaivilas proudly appeals to guests who believe that there cannot be too much luxury.

Shiv Niwas Palace
www.hrhhotels.com

The City Palace, Udaipur.
Ph: 0294 2528016

Owned and run by Shri Arvind Singh Mewar, the 76th Maharana of Udaipur, this hotel was originally a royal residence and used for private guests. It is located at the southern end of the palace complex and there are now 17 suites with private terraces. *An ideal spot to enjoy afternoon tea after touring the palace.*

Indian Romance

UDAIPUR –
City of Dawn

Founded in 1567, is one of the most spectacular places in India. It is set on magical lakes, surrounded by hills and dotted with marble palaces, hibiscus-laden gardens and fountain pavilions.

Where to stay

Devi Garh
www.deviresorts.com

Delwara, NH-8, Nr Eklingji, Nathdwara, District Rajsamand
Ph: 02953 289 211

If I was choosing just one place for a romantic Indian escape, Devi Garh is it. Nestled in the Aravali hills since the 18th-century, this Fort Palace in the village of Delwara, has been restored and rebuilt with wonderful sensitivity. The hotel was conceived as a place where the past meets the future. This luxury hotel comprises 39 suites with an emphasis on contemporary design and detail, using local materials. The pool is spectacular, spa treatments and yoga sessions can be arranged. The hotel has many wonderful suggestions for activities, horse or camel safaris, kite flying, sun-rise walks to temples, champagne sunset picnics with Dom Perignon and the most romantic of all, a private dinner for two on a private balcony high up on the fort serenaded with musicians. *Amazing.*

Located 28km northeast of Udaipur, Devi Garh is a scenic 45 min drive from the city. The garden suites are absolutely lovely and cost US$500 during the peak season. Suites in the palace begin at US$850 and are truly spectacular, each with unique features and stunning interiors.

Taj Lake Palace

www.tajhotels.com

Tel: 0294 2428800

This famous hotel is located on an island in the middle of Lake Pichola. *Made of white marble and mosaic, it is said to rival the Taj Mahal in beauty.* Converted into a hotel in 1963, the Taj Group now runs this ever-popular 83 rooms and suites property. The bar is a lovely place for afternoon tea or drinks.

Best Experience

City Palace

The well-fortified City Palace is a majestic white monument perched high up on a hill and is now a museum. Interesting, opulent and spectacular views.

Eklingji Temple

On the way to Devi Garh from Udaipur is this stunning temple with exquisite carving. The Maharana and his family continue to worship here weekly.

Fabulous – What to buy

The narrow lanes of Udaipur are crowded with brightly coloured stalls selling local art and craft. Best known for leather products, jewellery, rug weaving and marble work. Wander along until something catches your eye and then have an authentic haggling experience.

Devi Garh Shop

Daily 7am-7pm.

Truly fabulous. There is a beautiful curated collection of fashion, accessories and homewares. Local craft, contemporary Indian design and vintage pieces in a soothing fixed price environment.

Seva Mandir

Old Fatehpura, Udaipur (North-West Udaipur, nr Police Station off Fatehpura Circle).
Ph: 0294 2451 041, 0294 2450 960
Mon to Sat 9am-6pm.

This non-government voluntary organisation works on local, rural and tribal development issues and this small shop has a selection of lovely embroidered and block-printed textiles.

How to Get There

Udaipur's Dabok airport is well-connected to Mumbai with daily flights operated by Jet Airways and Indian Airlines. The flying time from to Mumbai is 75 mins.

Getting Around

Local taxis are easily available from the airport or the hotel can organise private cars. Devi Garh has some spectacular old *Ambassadors.*

Film

The James Bond Movie *Octopussy* was filmed here.

Vineyard
NASHIK –
The Wine Capital
of India

Nashik is known as the Varanassi of the East. The Godavari river flows through the town, many temples adorn the banks of the river and it is one of the four cities that hosts the massive Sinhastha Kumbh Mela once every twelve years.

In recent times, Nashik has become more famous as the wine capital of India. Though Scotch has long-been the tipple of choice and marker of social standing in the Indian social set, wine is now gaining real momentum, with consumption increasing by over 25% per annum.

Indians currently drink ten million bottles of wine a year; this is expected to double by 2010. There are approx 2,500 acres of grapevine under cultivation and about 40 wineries. A large concentration of these are located in Nashik.

Wine tourism is still in its infancy; but if you are interested in both wine and enjoying peaceful scenery, this adventure is recommended.

Best Experience
Sula Nashik Estate Winery & Tasting Room
www.sulawines.com

Gat No. 35/2, Govardhan, Gangapur-Savargaon Rd.
0253 223 1663, 0253 223 1720
Daily 11am - 10pm (11pm on Fri and Sat)
Tours 11.30am - 5.30pm.
(A late afternoon tour, followed by sunset drinks is the ideal timing).

Sula released wines in 2000 and since then has gained a global reputation as one of India's premium wine brands. Founder Rajeev Samant is an excellent ambassador for this new industry and his wines are in the finest restaurants around the world and at glamorous parties, including Liz Hurley's 40th birthday in London.

Rajeev quit his hi-tech Silicon Valley job in 1993 to start the Sula winery on his 30-acre family estate. Nashik is India's largest grape-growing region, but had traditionally never been used to grow wine grapes. In 1997, he planted French Sauvignon Blanc and Californian Chenin Blanc. Sula now has 400 acres under plantation, both in Nashik as well as in nearby Dindori.

The Dindori Reserve Shiraz, regarded as one of India's best wines.

The winery, located 40 mins out of town, has educational tours, which conclude with a tutored tasting of five wines. This *'beginners'* tasting costs Rs.100. *The Tasting Room*, the first visitor centre at an Indian winery, is a 2,000 sq.ft. modern purpose-built space, showcasing wines and merchandise for sale. The balcony bar has spectacular views of the vineyards and the surrounding lakes and hills and is a perfect place to enjoy the wines, served by the glass or by the bottle, accompanied by a cheese platter.

Where to stay

Taj Residency

www.tajhotels.com

P 17, Midc, Ambad, Mumbai-Agra Rd.

Ph: 0253 660 4499

The best hotel in town is the twelve-year-old Taj Residency. This 68-roomed hotel is a business hotel that has serviced the industrial city of Nashik. The hotel is only just adjusting to vineyard tourism and is beginning to integrate this into the experience offering local wines and some tasting dinners.

Set in 11 acres of garden, the hotel has a large swimming pool. The superior rooms have balconies, marble floors and are a bit bigger than standard rooms.

Beyond

www.sulawines.com/tastingroom/index.htm#beyond

Ph: (0)99700 90010

In November 2007, Sula opened a bungalow called 'Beyond' in their vineyards. The Bungalow overlooks Gangapur lake and has three large master bedrooms with private balconies and lounge areas, a small pool and extensive lawns. Cycles and kayaks are available. An in-house chef prepares all meals using organic ingredients from the Sula kitchen garden. Rates are Rs.20,000 plus tax per night on the weekend and Rs.16,000 plus tax for weekdays. This rate includes accommodation and all meals for up to six people plus a tour and tasting at Sula.

How to Get There

Nashik is about 180 km north-east of Mumbai – a journey of 3 to 4 hours by car or train.

Shirdi Sai Baba

Located about 100kms away from Nashik, Shirdi is a holy place for the mystic Saint Sai Baba who lived and died here and he promised the end of suffering for those who step on Shirdi soil. *After Tirupati it is the most visited pilgrim place in India.* An interesting and powerful place to visit.

Plan to reach here by 11am and gain access to the noon *darshan*, the ritual prayers at the tomb side. Thursdays are particularly auspicious. Foreigners can head to the VIP counter and gain special access.

Book

Shirdi Sai Baba (by Ashish Mohan Khokar, 2004). The author writes for the *Times of India* and has published over 30 books on Indian arts and spirituality. This small photographic volume is an excellent reference.

. Temple

AJANTA & ELLORA

Aurangabad is the jumping-off point for two of India's most spectacular World Heritage sites, the caves of Ajanta and Ellora. Aurangabad itself has little to offer, however, *Ajanta and Ellora may well be one of your most memorable experiences in India.* These sites sit alongside the Taj in Agra, the ruined city of Hampi and the temples of Khajuraho as *'must-see'* wonders of India. .

Where to stay

Taj Residency
www.tajhotels.com

8 N 12, Cidco, Rouja Bagh, Aurangabad.
Ph: 0240 6613 737

Located in the city centre, this 66-room hotel has a large pool and pretty gardens. This is the most upscale choice in the city, predominantly used as business hotel in the city and staffed by the training college next door. All of the rooms have *'sit-outs'* (small terraces), some have swings. The deluxe rooms are more modern and have marble floors, 312 is the best deluxe suite with a large bathtub and a good pool view. A reliable, if not particularly interesting, experience.

The Meadows
www.themeadowsresort.com
Gat. No. 135 & 136, Village Mitmita.
Ph: 0240 2677312-21

Over 40 comfortable modern cottages are scattered across 13 acres of landscaped gardens. Reasonable prices and considerate staff make this out-of-town resort a real alternative for a restful stay. The restaurant has both indoor and outdoor service, and it is nice to sit by the pool in the evening. Ask the chef for local specialities.

Best Experience

The Caves
My recommendation is to take two days to see the caves, as it is possible to become caved-out in one day! I would do them in chronological order, starting with Ajanta first. Travelling by private vehicle gives you maximum flexibility in terms of timing and is more relaxing than the government tour buses. Take your own torch and water.

Ajanta
Located 107kms out of Aurangabad. Open from 9.30am to 5.30pm. Closed Mondays. Rs.250 for foreigners, Rs.10 for Indian citizens.

It is believed that a group of Buddhist monks came to this remote area in the 2nd-century BC and began to carve the monolithic caves. Over the next 900 years, five *chaityas* (temples) and 25 *viharas* (monsasteries) were started, before the site was abandoned in favour of Ellora. It is worth taking a guide at the caves, like Mr Patil, who has been telling the stories and sharing the secrets of the caves for the last 30 years. He showed me the ceiling in *'cave 2'* with its painted-cloth canopy, complete with uneven ripple, just like a true tent canopy that moves with the wind.

Ellora

26kms from Aurangabad – Open sunrise to
sunset. Closed Tuesdays. Rs.250 for foreigners,
Rs.10 for Indian citizens.

A highly-remarkable series of 34 rock caves
and temples excavated from the crescent
shaped Charnadari Hill, carved over five
centuries by monks of three faiths.

There are 12 Buddhist caves, 17 Hindu ones
and five Jain in chronological order dating
from the 7th-century. The most splendid
of the whole series is the Kailas, a perfect,
profusely-carved, Dravidian-style temple.

This amazing temple rivals the actual Mt
Kailas in Western Tibet in terms of grandeur
and beauty. A *'must-see'*.

Daulatabad Fort

26kms from Aurangabad. Daily sunrise to sunset.

Once known as Devgiri, hill of the gods,
this 13th-century fortress is half-way between
Aurangabad and the Ellora Caves and offers
spectacular views to those that make the
hour-long trek to the citadel at the top.

Set on a natural hill, the fort has a series of
ingenious mazes and a string of booby traps,
*ideal for enthusiasts of 'Harry Potter' and 'Boys Own'
Stories.* Cross the moat, and through the spiked
doorways and along passageways so pitch-
black that you need to tip the torch bearer to
be shown the way ahead. *Great fun and not to
be missed.*

How to Get There

There are daily flights
to and from Mumbai on
Indian Airlines, Jet Airways
and Air Deccan. Jet has
two flights per day, which
enables you to arrive early
morning and spend just one
night and two full days at
the caves, departing on the
evening of the second day.

When to go

The caves are best during
the cooler winter months or
during the monsoon, when
the area is lush and green.

Getting Around

Your hotel will arrange
a local car service. *Avoid
Classic Travel due to unreliable
cars and drivers.* Expect to pay
Rs.2,000 for the round-trip
to Ajanta and Rs.1,000 for
the round-trip to Ellora
and Daulatabad.

Book

India (by Stanley Wolpert,
2005 edition). A distillation
of UCLA's great historian of
a lifetime of learning about
India with a great chapter on
the caves.

'Bombay is beautiful not for its big buildings, for most of them hide squalid poverty and dirt, nor for its wealth, for most of it is derived from the blood of the masses, but for its world-renowned generosity'.

Mahatma Gandhi, Bombay, 1921

LOVE TRAVEL GUIDES
www.Lovetravelguides.com

VII ESSENTIAL
Living:

Mumbaikars have a legendary generosity of spirit, in evidence most recently when they faced the severe Monsoon floods of 2005 and the bombings of 2006. The city pulls together in a completely cohesive way. On a daily scale, the warmth and friendliness of the people makes visiting the city a delight. Meeting and engaging with local Mumbaikars, including your taxi driver, is the best way to relate to the city.

AUTOMOBILES
Taxis

The black and yellow Mumbai taxi, based on a 1950s Fiat, is an iconic image of the city. Over 50,000 of these individually decorated taxis cover the city and are easy to hail. The drivers are normally pretty good and use the meter reading. Note that a 25% extra charge is levied after midnight.

Plus there are over 7,000 silver and blue air-conditioned, Cool Cabs, which cost about 50% more. These can be found at ranks of major hotels or can be ordered via Ph: 2824 6216 and 2490 5151.

There are two premium taxi services offering A/C cars at metered rates. The Esteem service uses Olive green Mauti Esteem cars and can be reached on Ph: 4422 4422. The Mumbai Gold Cabs use both Indigo Marina cars and Maruti Esteem cars and can be reached on Ph: 3244 3333.

Car Services

All hotels offer comfortable car services; the drivers speak better English than those in taxis, but come at five-star prices. For example, a trip to the airport at a hotel price can be close to Rs.3,000 (or close to Rs.6,000 for a Mercedes) instead of Rs.500 in an A/C taxi.

When you hire a car for out-of-town trips, it comes with the services of the driver. Most companies will quote a per km rate, based on the size of car and whether you want A/C or not. Whilst the idea of tootling around India in an old *Ambassador* is a romantic one, the comfort of a *Toyota Qualis* for a few extra rupees per km wins out. Aruna Travels comes highly recommended by many expats, call Ph: 2495 4617 or 2496 8844.

Travel Tip

Find a taxi driver you like and keep him.

I found my taxi driver in the cab rank at the Taj Mahal Hotel some three years ago, and he is a legend –
Mr Harish *is contactable on (0)98926 95669 His A/C cab is immaculate, his English very good and his knowledge of the city unbeatable.*

Betsy Karel, the photographer of the wonderful book 'Bombay Jadoo', gives her long-time taxi driver –
Mr Happy *– an unqualified 7 stars. He can be reached on (0)92243 43292*

Taxi

Auto Rickshaws

These three-wheelers are only allowed north of the Mahim creek, so they start in Bandra and continue north. There are thousands of these buzzy little *'ricks'* or *'autos'* plying the suburban roads. They are the fastest way to get about and are cheap albeit noisy. They have metres, often out-of-date, and the driver will refer to a conversion chart. After midnight add 25%.

PLANES

Mumbai Airport is also known as Chhatrapati Shivaji International Airport and has a domestic site (Terminal 1A and 1B) and an international complex (Terminal 2A and 2C). It is the busiest airport in the country with over 36 international airlines and over ten domestic airlines flying in and out of Mumbai.

Mumbai's domestic airport is located at Santacruz, some 26kms from South Mumbai. There is no public transport to and from the airport so cars are the only option. At minimum it will take one hour to reach and in busy traffic up to two hours one-way.

The international airport is further north at Sahar Village, some 30kms from South Mumbai and 4kms from the Domestic Airport. A shuttle exists between the two, allow 30 mins to connect from one to the other.

Domestically, the traditional airlines, Indian and Jet Airways have been joined by Kingfisher (likened to Virgin) and a plethora of low cost carriers including Jet Lite, Air Deccan, Go Air, Indigo, and Spice Jet.

Two useful websites to check out the best fares for domestic travel are:
www.travelguru.com
www.india.makemytrip.com

The first train journey in India took place in 1853 from Bombay to Thane and carried 400 people. The Indian railway is now legendary and is one of the largest in the world.

Mumbai has an efficient but overcrowded suburban rail system that transports over 6 million people per day

TRAINS

The main station is VT Victoria Terminus, renamed Chhatrapti Shivaji Terminus, but still affectionately known as VT. *This station, built in 1808, is the busiest in India and is a World Heritage site.*

The local trains run on three separate lines, the *Western* line from Churchgate Station, the *Harbour* line and the *Central* line from VT Station, and operate between 3.30am and 1am

Avoid travelling during peak times (7am - 11am, 4pm - 9pm) when the trains are so crowded that it seems more people are hanging on the outside than are packed inside. Tickets are only sold at railway counters and are cheap, less than Rs.100 for first-class.

Mumbai has excellent rail links to the rest of the country and different classes of travel are available. Book through the hotel concierge or E-tickets can now be booked on line at ***www.irctc.co.in***

Communicating

LANGUAGE

Marathi is the official language of Mumbai, however English and Hindi are widely used. Public signs and public announcements are in English and it is readily understood.

Mumbaikars welcome efforts to communicate in Indian languages and a simple *Namaskar*, ('Hello' in Marathi) or *Shukria* ('Thank you' in Hindi) will generate warmth. However to really connect one would use the language of the streets, *Bambaiyia Hindi*.

People from every part of India live together in Mumbai. This inter-mingling has created a language affectionately called *Bambaiya Hindi*, also known as *Mumbaiyya*. It has a Hindi/Urdu as a base, but includes words and pronunciations from other languages such as English, Marathi and Gujarati, as well as languages from South India, such as Tamil. The colourful phrases in Bambaiya Hindi are not the language of the upper classes, but of the street.

Below are the commonly spoken words in Bambaiya Hindi (or Bhindi, which is also the word for okra!) used by Bombaywallas in daily life.

Yaar (yaar) – Everyone is called *'yaar'* or friend in Mumbai. *'Yaar'* is used in English conversations too, as in, *'No, yaar, not today'*.

Saala (sah-lah) – Literally meaning *'wife's brother'*... but in Bombay it is used in every context... when friends meet and greet then it is *'kya saala kaisa hai'*... (Hey, man, how are you?) when angry *'abey saala... phoot na'*... (Hey, man, get lost) in fact this is the most commonly used word in Bombay (after *yaar*)... and can be used when you are happy/sad/depressed/angry/shy/vulgar/teasing and when there is nothing else to say, then use a *saala*.

Chikna (chick-nah)
Stands for any good-looking fellow. Chikna actually means smooth. *'Kya, chikna. Kaisa hai?'* (Hey, good-looking, how are you?).

Haila (hi-lah)
This originated from *'Hai Allah'* and translates to *'Oh God'*. *'Haila, kya item hai!'* translates to *'My god, she's really cool!'*

Jhakaas (jhu-kaas)
Superb. Excellent. *'Ekdum jhakaas'* would mean *'too good'*.

Hajaam dhakkan (hujj-aam dhu-kkun)
'Hajaam' in its true sense would mean a barber. Dhakkan literally means *'lid'*. It refers to anyone with a poor intellect, an idiot. *'Dhakkan samjha hai, kya?'* would mean *'Do you think I am dumb?'*

Shana (shah-nah)
Literal meaning in Marathi means wise... but mostly used in sarcastic way like *'tu kya shana hai kya?'* (You think you are very smart, do you?).

131

Travel Tip

Bring a handful of passport pics with you; they are needed for all official transactions and on all forms.

PHONE CALLS & EMAIL

Mobile Phones

India Country Code

The country code for India is +91

Mumbai Area Code

The Mumbai dialling code is 022

If you are dialling a Mumbai landline number from a mobile phone, you need to add 022 before the 8-digit number.

When dialling from a Mumbai landline or mobile, if you are dialling an outside of Mumbai mobile phone, add a *'0'* before the number.

Mumbai lives on the mobile phone. The 'missed call' is an art form and is a way of communicating in itself. People will call and expect a return call, particularly drivers and shops that do not want to clock up the call charge. People don't use voicemail systems, even if available and texting is hugely popular.

If you are visiting for any time, it is easy to get a local SIM card and use a prepaid service. You will need to take your passport and two passport-size pictures into any of the major phone companies such as Hutch, Reliance, or Airtel.

Email & Internet Services

Internet cafés are everywhere and are cheap. Wireless Internet access is expanding rapidly and is available at many hotels and the airport. Some cafés offer wireless, including Indigo Deli *(pg21)*.

USEFUL & EMERGENCY NO's

Directory Enquiries

Just Dial is a very useful free service. It is an operator-assisted telephone search engine and they can find *'almost'* everything for you with a name, category and ideally, location. They will ask for your number and/or email. The 24-hour info line is Ph: 022 3999 9999.

Emergency

Police
Ph: 100

Fire
Ph: 101

Ambulance
Ph: 102

Hospitals

24-hour accident and emergency services.

Note: If possible, it is best to transport the patient directly to the emergency department of a hospital, as it will save time waiting for the ambulance to navigate Mumbai traffic, few people give way to sirens and flashing lights in the city

⑦ Bombay Hospital
www.bombayhospital.com

12 Marine Lines.
Ph: 2206 7676 ext 260

⑭ Breach Candy Hospital
www.breachcandyhospital.org

60A Bhulabhai Desai Rd.
Ph: 2367 1888, 2367 2888
Casualty Direct: 2366 7809

㉑ Lilavati Hospital
www.lilavatihospital.com

A791 Bandra Reclamation.
Ph: 2643 8281, 2643 8282

Spending

BANKING, NEGOTIATING & TIPPING

ATM's are everywhere, including Citibank and HSBC, and are the easiest way of getting local currency. Travellers' checks are fine at hotels.

The Rupee (abbreviated as Rs.) is the currency and at the time of writing
USD $1 = Rs.39;
GBP = Rs.79;
Euro 1 = Rs.57;
Aus $1 = Rs.34.

In big shops, prices are normally fixed; in markets and street stalls, haggling is normal. A request for *'best price'* and some good-hearted *'to-ing'* and *'fro-ing'* can see a reduction in the asking price – as usual, decide what you think is good value.

Tipping is expected, 10% is normal in a restaurant and if tipping people directly just small amounts, up to Rs.50, is fine. In India, one tips to open doors and get things done; this incentive-based tipping necessitates slightly higher payments.

Blending In

A CULTURAL VADE MECUM

The Headshake

We may be used to a nodding motion up-and-down signifying *'yes'* and a shaking from side-to-side meaning *'no'*, but in India the most famous gesture is that of the *'rotational headshake'*. This can mean anything and everything – with a smile it may be *'yes'*; or it may be *'maybe'*; or in many cases it could mean *'I couldn't care less'*... and on the subject of heads, never touch one – (any)one's head is considered sacred.

Hands & Feet

Whilst shaking hands with men is common, it is rude to touch an Indian woman and they may feel uncomfortable. Never use your left hand for anything; it is considered unclean. Hand-washing is hygienic and there can never be too much of it; most restaurants will have a special place for this pre- and post- a meal. Do not point with your finger; use your chin. In many homes it is customary to remove your footwear (*'chappals'* is the local word) upon entering. Do what your hosts do and make sure your feet and shoes do not touch anybody or anything; they are also considered unclean.

No Saying No

Indians are unlikely to ever say *'no'*; they would rather tell you a lie than upset you or disagree with you. This is true in an auto and can result in getting very lost and equally true in high-level business dealings and intimate personal relationships. Similarly, a direct *'no'* from you is considered harsh. In addition, *'I don't know'* doesn't feature in the Indian vocabulary and often you will be given the answer that they think you want to hear; *'Yes, the temple is that way'* may be an outright lie or they simply may not have a clue.

The Art of Conversation

Be prepared for a full and immediate interrogation of your personal life from anyone – this polite *'time pass'* conversation knows no boundaries. However, be careful in navigating sensitive topics that may embarrass Indians such as dowries, female infanticide, poverty, and corruption. Note: discussing sex falls into this category, as do affairs and divorce. Read 'Page Three' for all the gossip!

Smoking, Drinking & Drugs

All of these activities are on the rise in India. *Bidis* are the small, local cigarettes made of cheap tobacco and it is a good idea to avoid them. Indian cigarettes are cheap and can be bought individually and cigarette papers, (Rizla papers) are available. Indian beer is good and plentiful and served widely. Indians enjoy drinking (however, it is normally done before the meal). In fact, when the meal is served it's often the signal to go home. Drugs are illegal and available; be very careful.

Kissing & Cuddling

Public displays of affection between the sexes are simply a no-no and physical contact is disapproved. However, Indian men will often hold hands as a symbol of friendship – it doesn't mean they are gay. Homosexuality is a taboo subject in India and technically remains a criminal act under the Indian penal code but there is growing tolerance and acceptance, especially in the cities.

Dressing & Undressing

Outside of nightclubs, Indians are conservative in clothing and it's important that women are modest. This means not exposing cleavage and shoulders, which are considered quite erotic by Indian men. Adopting the local dress is an easy solution; wearing a *kurta* (tunic) over pants is ideal and a *dupatta* (long scarf) is short-hand for modesty and virtue. Be careful not to 'underdress' – whilst business attire is more casual, socially, there is a tendency to dress up.

Spiritual Sensitivity

India is the home of spirituality and the major religions are practised with fervour. Be aware of the sacredness of the cow, avoid mentioning beef, let alone eating it – and avoid wearing cowhide products wherever possible around Hindus (over 80% of the population). When visiting temples look and learn – follow the example of others by removing footwear, walking clockwise, wearing conservative clothing, and cause minimal interference talking or taking photographs.

Indian Standard (stretchable) time (IST)

This term refers to the loose notion of time-keeping in India. Western sensibility around time is not understood and it can be very rude to hurry people.

Similarly, being *'pushy'* and aggressive rarely works and is looked down upon. While this form of behaviour may, in the short term, get you what you want, it is not the best way to *'spread the love'*.

Red, Red Tape

Indian bureaucracy is legendary and slowness, delays, queues and paperwork are a fact of life in a country of over a billion people – one of the few places in the world still using carbon paper.

Think of this as an opportunity to work on the virtues of tolerance and patience, perhaps!!

Reading

India was the star attraction of the world biggest bookfair this year in Frankfurt. Rightly so, the quality and quantity of Indian literature is outstanding. Enjoy these marvellous books:

BOOKS

Bombay, meri jaan, Writings on Mumbai edited by Jerry Pinto and Naresh Fernandes, 2003.

Fiction

A Fine Balance by Rohinton Mistry, 1995.

Ravan and Eddie by Kiran Nagarkar, 1995.

Love and Longing in Bombay by Vikram Chandra, 1997.

The Ground Beneath Her Feet by Salman Rushdie, 2000.

Death of Vishnu by Manil Suri, 2001.

Shantaram by Gregory David Roberts, 2003.

Sacred Games by Vikram Chandra, 2006.

Non-Fiction

City of Gold, The Biography of Bombay by Gillian Tindall, 1982. Updated 1992.

Once was Bombay by Pinky Virani, 1999.

Rediscovering Dharavi by Kalpana Sharma, 2000.

The Holy Cow and other Indian Stories by Tarun Chopra, 2000.

The Mumbai Factfile by Derek O'Brien, 2003.

Maximum City. Bombay Lost and Found by Suketu Mehta 2004.

Culture Smart India – A quick guide to customs & etiquette 2003, revised 2004, 2005.

Culture Shock! India: A Survival Guide to Customs and Etiquette by Gitanjali Kolanad, 2005.

Busy Bee Best of Behram Contractors' columns from Afternoon Despatch newspaper.

Guide Books

Namaskar Mumbai. At home in Mumbai, a guide to the international community. 2nd edition, 2006. This useful directory is essential for people coming to live in the city: *www.mumbaiconnexions.com* or *www.awcbombay.com*

Fort Walks
by Sharada Dwivedi and Rahul Mehrotra, 1999.

52 Weekend Breaks from Mumbai
by Outlook Traveller, 2003 (reprinted 2006).

Lonely Planet Best of Mumbai
by Joe Bindloss, 2006.

Lonely Planet Citiscape
Mumbai by Joe Bindloss, 2006.

Time Out Mumbai and Goa 2006.

Time Out Kids' Guide 2007.

Times Food Guide 2007
by Rashmi Uday Singh.

Wallpaper City Guide: Mumbai 2007.

Photography/Coffee Table Books

Bombay to Mumbai, Changing perspectives
edited by Pauline Rohatgi, Pheroza Godrej and Rahul Mehrotra, 1997.

Bombay Jadoo
by Photographer Betsy Karel, 2007.

Louis Vuitton Mumbai Scrapbook.
A collection of watercolours of Mumbai images by French Artist Florine Asch.

NEWSPAPERS

The biggest selling English language newspaper is *The Times of India*. Other dailies include *The Indian Express*, *The Asian Age* and *The Hindustan Times*.

The afternoon tabloids are *The Afternoon Dispatch and Courier* and *Mid-Day*.

All papers are only a few rupees and are a great insight into the culture of the city.

MAGAZINES

Time Out is an excellent fortnightly magazine listing all the current events in the city: *www.timeoutmumbai.net*

Upper Crust Magazine is based in Mumbai and is India's premier gourmet magazine. It comes out every two months and is an excellent source of information for the city and for travel across India.

WEBSITES

Mumbai tourist information site: *www.explocity.com/Mumbai*

Mumbai reference site: *www.mumbainet.com*

Mumbai news portal: *www.mumbai-central.com*

Notes

VIIIa SLEEPING
SoBo Staying:

India has experienced double-digit growth in foreign tourism numbers, middle-class domestic travel has increased significantly, and in the last decade, there has been a major shift in the profile of hotel users from leisure to business travellers.

Hence, there is intense pressure on hotel rooms that has sent room prices skyrocketing (Mumbai's average room rate in a five-star hotel now sits at USD$400).

My advice – make reservations early and look for special promotions and packages; plus, Club Rooms offer good value.

NoBo Staying:
(pg143)

Nesting & Resting

HERITAGE

① Taj Mahal Palace & Tower
www.tajhotels.com

Apollo Bunder, Colaba.
Ph 6665 3366

The most-famous and most-loved hotel in the city. Built in 1903 by Jamshedji Tata who, after he was refused entry to a European hotel, decided to create the most beautiful hotel in the city, with sweeping views of the Arabian Sea. The tower was built in 1972 bringing the number of rooms and suites to 582. A high-profile hotel, famous guests include Bill Clinton, Elton John, John Lennon and Yoko Ono. Liz Hurley and Arun Nair recently celebrated their wedding in the honeymoon suite, the Bell Tower. The swimming pool is legendary and is the best in India, worth staying just for this!

Best Room *The sea facing Taj clubrooms* on the fifth and sixth floors of the heritage wing are superb for sunrise and represent good value. Services include in-room check-in, butler service, airport pick-up-and-drop, breakfast, high tea, cocktails and complimentary Internet access at the club. The Diplomat Luxury suite is wonderful and is one of only four luxury suites that have sea views.

The Taj Mahal Palace & Tower

BUSINESS

③ Oberoi
www.oberoihotels.com

Nariman Point.
Ph: 6632 5757

This is an important hotel in the business life of the city. Opened in 1986 with over 300 rooms, the hotel is quietly opulent and is located in the business district with superb views overlooking the Arabian Sea and along the *"Queen's Necklace".* The restaurants are sleek, expensive and are desired venues for business entertaining. Bill Clinton, Bill Gates, Richard Gere, Jack Welch and Rupert Murdoch have all stayed in the Kohinoor Suite, which is an oasis of calm.

Best Room *The luxury sea-facing rooms* include airport transfers and breakfast and, given these extras, are about the same price as the base category.

③ Hilton Towers
www.hilton.com

Nariman Point.
Ph 6632 4343

The biggest hotel in South Bombay, with 541 rooms, is a delightful surprise. The property is 34-years-old and the public areas look a little dated, but the renovated rooms are spectacular and represent good value. The pool is good and the restaurants and bars popular. Silhouette is an excellent salon, located on pool level *(pg88)*.

Best Room *Hilton executive floors* (27, 28, 29) have spectacular views of the Arabian Sea or the Harbour. The lounge is located on the 28th and is great place for a sunset cocktail. The rate for these rooms includes plenty of extras and is good value.

⑯ ITC, Grand Central Hotel
www.itcwelcomgroup.com

287 Dr. B. Ambedkar Rd, Parel.
Ph: 2410 1010

Built in 2004, this 242-room hotel is 30 floors high and has panoramic views of Mumbai's sprawling metropolis. This hotel was the pioneer in the central Mumbai business district and its location is the main attraction. The western view across to the Worli Sea Face is my preferred outlook with the ocean visible in the distance.

Best Room *ITC One rooms*, located on high floors, are actually suites and represent value given the extra space and amenities. Room 2312 has a west view and is on a non-smoking floor.

② Taj President
www.tajhotels.com

90 Cuffe Parade, Colaba.
Ph 6665 0808

This mid-size hotel (292 rooms) has a loyal business clientele and is in process of being updated. The restaurants are much-admired.

Best Room *Higher floors give the best views.* Ask for sea facing, there is no extra cost for this.

BOUTIQUE

⑤ Intercontinental
www.mumbai.
intercontinental.com

135 Marine Drive.
Ph 3987 9676

This hotel has an intimate personal scale with only 58 rooms across the six floors. The rooms are well designed and many have spectacular views, perfect for sunset. Thoughtful services include a complimentary 20 min in-room massage, room aroma selection and a pillow and quilt menu. The small rooftop pool and exercise studio are very hip. The hotel has the best bar in town, ***The Dome (pg33)***.

Best Room *Deluxe sea fronts are the best;* ask for 224, 225, 226, 227, 334, 335, 336, or 337. Make sure to avoid side-views; you may end up looking on to a building wall. The deluxe bay view suites are great, the higher the better; room 442 is recommended and the deluxe corner suite is magnificent, room 663.

We recommend you support organisations that are socially and/or environmentally sustainable, identified here with the Conscious Travel symbol (pg149)

BOUTIQUÉ (CONT'D)

❶ Gordon House Hotel

www.ghhotel.com

5 Battery Street, Apollo Bunder, Colaba.
Ph: 2287 1122

Presented as the only boutique hotel in the city with 28 rooms and one suite. Located in Colaba, close to the Taj Hotel and just around the corner from Indigo Deli. The room décor is Country Cottage, Mediterranean or Swedish. Certainly not my choice for an authentic experience! It is cheaper than nearby five-star hotels, but a good deal from one of them could get you a matching price and would be better.

Best Room *One at the front of the hotel for light and on a higher floor to minimise the noise* from the nightclub in the hotel.

CONTEMPORARY

⑰ Four Seasons

www.fourseasons.com

114 Dr E Moses Road, Worli.
Ph: 2481 8000

🖐 *The eagerly anticipated opening of Mumbai's latest luxury hotel will take place in April 2008.* The contemporary-designed 202 guest rooms and suites showcase the views of the Mumbai skyline through floor-to-ceiling windows and are the largest accommodation in the city. The hotel team has been extremely active in engaging with the city in a meaningful way so that the experience can be shared with guests. They are also implementing an active corporate social responsibility programme within the local community.

BUDGET

❶ Ascot Hotel

38 Garden Rd. Colaba.
Ph: 6638 5566

Refurbished three years ago this moderate hotel is a good choice. There are 30 modern rooms with wooden floors, neutral tones, desks with broadband Internet access. It is half the price of Gordon House and simply, better.

Best Room *Choose one the deluxe rooms.* They are very spacious, only cost Rs.500 more than a standard room and are located at front of hotel overlooking the leafy street.

VIIIb SLEEPING

NoBo Staying:

Over the last few years,
an extra 1,200
five-star rooms have
become available
in Mumbai,
predominantly in
NoBo, to service
the area's growing
commercial
requirements and
the needs of national
and international
travellers to be close
to the airports.

The next spurt of
hotel growth will be in
Navi Mumbai to meet
the needs of the IT
industry and to service
the new airport.

SoBo Staying:
(pg139)

FIVE-STAR & ABOVE

㉑ Taj Lands End

www.tajhotels.com

Bandstand, Bandra.
Ph: 6668 1234

This 18-storey business hotel has 368 rooms, some of which are the largest in the city. The hotel has good restaurants and is hugely popular for functions and events.

Best Room *The Taj clubrooms on the 21st floor* in B Block have sea views. Ask for rooms ending in /27, /29, /31, /33, and /35.

However, the cityscape bay view across the pool has its own charm, looking across the gardens to the harbour with the new bridge.

The Harbour Presidential Suite on the 21st floor is stunning as are the Luxury Suites and Grand Luxury Suites on the 20th and 21st floors. The endless ocean view is relaxing and puts you in a true vacation mode.

㉒ JW Marriott

www.marriotthotels.com

Juhu Tara Rd.
Ph: 6693 3000

High glitz and glam. This prestigious hotel is the most grand and modern hotel in the Juhu area. It is like a resort, with 355 rooms and suites, many with fabulous views across the three swimming pools to the golden beach.

The hotel is full of Bollywood dreams. Stars and starlets, and partygoers often have all 355 suites booked. The restaurants are stylish and excellent; the nightclub is the hottest place in town. There is an exceptional spa and a small high-end shopping centre with the very good Bombay Baking Company Café and shop.

Best Room *The grand ocean suites are amazing with huge bathtubs that overlook the beach.* In terms of rooms, choose an executive superior room with a full ocean view and access to the club on the fourth-floor. Ask for 406, 408 and 410 or 506, 508, 510.

Sun'n'Sand
www.sunandsandhotel.com

39 Juhu Beach Rd.
Ph: 6693 8888, 2620 1811

Built in 1962, this was the first luxury hotel on Mumbai's iconic Juhu beach. Bollywood greats congregated in the bars, restaurants and rooms.

Unfortunately, there is no celebration of this wonderful legacy and what could be the best boutique gem in Bombay is merely a decent, good-value place to stay.

The 120 rooms are inconsistent in design and levels of renovation. The superior ocean facing rooms on a high floor are a good option. The seven luxury suites have global themes and all are ocean-facing with stunning views.

The **Kebab Hut** restaurant remains a popular institution and the **Aqua Spirit Bar (pg40)** is good. There is a salon and an authentic Ayurvedic spa.

Best Room *419, an executive room with ocean views, wooden floors and good bathtub.*

BUDGET

Iskcon Temple Guest House
www.iskconmumbai.com/guesthouse

Hare Krishna land, Juhu Church Rd, Juhu.
Ph: 2620 6860

The rooms are spacious, spotless and come with air-conditioning and balconies. There is no pressure to be a devotee and **Govinda** is an excellent vegetarian restaurant *(pg36)*. Great value, an air-conditioned double costs Rs.2,500.

Orchid

www.orchidhotel.com

Nehru Rd, Vile Parle (E).
Ph: 2616 4040

Asia's first and most-awarded eco hotel. The eco-friendly initiatives are excellent, however, the décor of the 245 rooms is drab. Best to use on departure, because on arrival you would need to drive a long way and do a U-turn to come back to the hotel.

The pool and spa are open to non-guests for a small fee.

Best Room *Club Privé rooms on the sixth floor overlook the runway for enthusiastic plane spotters.*

DOMESTIC AIRPORT

Grand Hyatt

www.grandhyattmumbai.com

Off Western Express Highway, Santacruz (E).
Ph: 6676 1234

Global and grand in scale. Mumbai's biggest hotel with 547 rooms and 147 serviced apartments.

This is a busy business and convention hotel located 5 mins from the Bandra-Kurla Complex, 15 mins from the Domestic Airport and 30 mins from the International Airport. The hotel is facility rich, with five restaurants; a spa/gym spread over 11,000 sq.ft.w and a high-end shopping mall.

Best Room *The verandah rooms on the club level.* The only opportunity for fresh air; ask for outdoor furniture.

INTERNATIONAL AIRPORT

Le Royal Meridien

www.lemeridien.com

Sahar Airport Rd, Andheri (E).
Ph: 2838 0000

This is a little gem. The boutique hotel opened in 2000, with just 171 rooms, now has a very loyal clientele.

The European décor is luxurious and sensuous with an overlay of colonial style celebrating India. The service is thoughtful from the airport collection by a butler in a Mercedes (waiting with a cold drink and a cold towel) to the in-room pillow menu and teddy bear on the bed.

They have a splendid aircrew room and Virgin Atlantic (amongst others) choose to stay here. The dining options are good and the bar is the best of the airport hotels. An intimate spa and gym is open to guests and non-guests from 6am - 10pm.

Best Room *The Royal Club rooms* have excellent complimentary services and are good value. Pool view is the best option.

Leela Kempinski
www.theleela.com

Sahar.
Ph: 6691 1234

The first five-star from the Leela Group established in 1987. The hotel is set in 11 acres of gardens and the pool is lovely. The 390 rooms have seen extensive upgrades over the last four years.

The lounge is a popular meeting spot and the poolside café is a relaxing. Good restaurants.

Best Room *The Royal Club rooms on the 6th, 7th and 8th floors.*

ITC Maratha
www.itcwelcomgroup.in

Sahar.
Ph: 2831 4444

The luxury property was built in 2000 and is decorated in grand Indian style. There are 386 rooms. Guests include heads-of-state, ambassadors, and corporates, British Airways flight crew and Shilpa Shetty.

This is widely-accepted as the *'gourmet hotel of Mumbai'* with some of the finest restaurants in the city. *(pg41).*

Best Room *ITC one and club tower rooms have exclusive club areas and complimentary breakfasts and drinks. Ask for a pool view.*

Hyatt Regency
www.mumbai.regency.hyatt.in

Sahar Airport Rd, Andheri (E).
Ph: 6696 1234

A modern hip hotel, sleek and cool, this 400-roomed property is constructed from glass and steel. It has the best pool, gym and spa facilities of any of the Airport hotels and it is open to non-guests *(pg95).*

Best Room *The Regency clubrooms include breakfast and transfers. Good value.*

Intercontinental, The Grand
www.intercontinental.com

Sahar Airport Rd.
Ph: 6699 2222

Built in 2004, this 369-roomed hotel has one of the largest atriums in the country. There is a 24-hour gym and pool and non-hotel guests can gain access for Rs.500.

Best Room *Any standard room overlooking the pool.*

LOVE TRAVEL FOUNDATION

Love Travel Guides is committed to 'Conscious Travel'. We aim to be Conscious of the society and country we are visiting and believe in contributing to it in a meaningful way.

Five per cent of the sales of this book will go to the Foundation to assist Conscious organisations and charities that undertake social and/or environmentally sustainable work in India.

We recommend supporting the socially and/or environmentally sustainable organisations highlighted in this book, as they make a significant contribution to livelihood support and improved living conditions in India.

They are identified throughout this book by this symbol...

IX SHARE THE LOVE
Helping:

**A quarter of the world's destitute live
in India.** Over 380 million Indians (35%
of the population) live below the poverty
line, subsisting on less than US$1 a day
and almost 80% of the total population
live on under US$2 a day.

Conversely, as India's economy grows,
(9.4% in fiscal 2006/2007), millionaires
are being created at a record rate and there
are now over 100,000. This is a 20%
increase on the previous year.

Bridging the gap between the 'two' Indias
is perhaps the greatest challenge facing the
country today – and for a visitor to come
to terms with. There is a rapidly-developing
middle class, but visitors should be sensitive
to the fact that wages are low and even a
middle-class family is likely living on less
than US$1,000 a month.

The majority of Indians continue to believe
in reincarnation and the concept of karma;
this appears to protect the country from open
distress about the poverty. However, charity
and giving back is an important part of
Indian life.

It can be hard to resist the pleas of a small
child or a handicapped person, but it is
important to know that many of the beggars
belong to rackets, and that by giving to them
you may make the situation worse. The
leader, who keeps the majority of the earn-
ings, will often inflict more mutilation on the
beggars to elicit greater sympathy and income.
It is best to give something consumable
(fruit, milk, clothes, medicines).

*It is recommended
for travellers to
contribute to reputable
charities in lieu
of giving to
the street beggars.*

*In Mumbai,
a good resource is*
**Mumbai
Connexions,**
*an expat group
that has been in
existence for over
30 years and
supports five
Mumbai charities.*

*For more
information go to:*
**www.mumbaicon-
nexions.com/
Charities.htm.**

X ALPHABETICAL INDEX
Finding by Name

XI AREA INDEX
Finding by Area

www.Lovetravelguides.com

XI AREA INDEX (CONT'D)
Finding by Area

Love Mumbai
Second Edition, 2008.

Researched, written, designed, set and proofread in India, Bali, Singapore and Australia; printed and handcrafted in India.

Publishing notes

Book printed and hand-bound by Papeterie, Delhi
www.papeterie.in

Printed on eco-friendly and non-bleached hand-made paper. The entire production process is child labour free.

Book cover developed in partnership with the fashion designer Sonam Dubal, Delhi
www.sonamdubal.com

Printed on traditional Tibetan raw silk, colloquially termed 'burrey' or 'tsen', which is hand-woven in South Assam, India.

Bookmark hand-crafted in Bangalore by Chandrashekar of Metaphor.
www.meta-phor.blogspot.com

Luxury Edition silk pouch designed by Sonali of Hidden Harmony, Bangalore

Made from Mysore Silk and Khadi handloom lining.

Book design and typography by David Terrazas and Jeremy Jones at ing group, Sydney, www.inggroup.com.au

Typeface selection was inspired by a mix of the 'old' and 'new' – set in Baskerville and Verdana.

Tale of Two Cities Essay by Anand Giridharadas, The International Herald Tribune, Bombay Bureau.

Illustrations by Sameer Kulavoor, Mumbai
www.sameerkulavoor.com

Map design, proofing and indexing by Dr Annapurna Garimella and Vinayak Varma of Jackfruit, Research & Design Pvt Ltd, Bangalore
www.jackfruitresearchdesign.com

LOVE TRAVEL GUIDES
www.Lovetravelguides.com

Editing
Shoshanna Kirk, Rebecca Poston and Nikki Mohan.

Content Contributions
Rushina Munshaw – Ghildiyal on Delicious and Knita Row on Essential. Shruti Singh on Gorgeous and Sleeping.

Thank You
Sue and Shauket, Krish and Nikki, Ajay and Knita, Suzie and Dave, Nari and Kadambri, Manjusha and Vikram, Amar, Avinash, Bob and Karan, Beate, Arnaz, Burjor, Debasis, Caje, Pablo, Abhay, Anu, Maithili, Jamini, Loulou, Hema, Sally, Diyva, Anita, A.D, James, Mekhla, Meher, Farzana, Rashida, Monica, Abha, Deepa, Shriti, Rekha, Sanjeev, Bhavna and Aparna, and many others, for their friendship and company, abundant suggestions and advice.

The staff at the Royal Bombay Yacht Club and the Cricket Club of India for making me feel so at home over the last three years.

Harish who graciously drove me all over the city whilst I drove him mad!

Chris and Ben, David T, Katrina and Ambrose who opened their homes to me and saw a little bit of work get done.

Barbara and Ramon, Anne, Caroline, Teresa, Sally, Angela, Richard, Dave, Juan, and Bob for joining me in the Mumbai Adventure.

About the author

Fiona Caulfield is a citizen of the world.

Born in Australia, she has lived in the UK, Canada and the USA, and is now resident in India.

She has a high profile global career as a futurist and branding consultant and is an avid traveller and explorer.

A self-confessed luxury vagabond, she has a discerning eye for the singular experiences that set a destination apart. This is her second book in the Love Travel Guide Indian series.

For more information visit or email:

www.lovetravelguides. com/about.htm

fiona@lovetravelguides.com

Notes